LOVE RULES

LOVE RULES

The Ten Commandments
for the 21st Century

Edited by

STUART BONNINGTON
JOAN MILNE

THE BANNER OF TRUTH TRUST

THE BANNER OF TRUTH TRUST
3 Murrayfield Road, Edinburgh EH12 6EL, UK
P.O. Box 621, Carlisle, PA 17013, USA

*

First published by the Church and Nation Committee
of the Presbyterian Church of Victoria, 2004

© The Presbyterian Church of Victoria, 2004

*

First Banner of Truth edition, 2007

ISBN 978 0 85151 957 9

*

Typeset in 11/15 pt Garamond at the
Banner of Truth Trust, Edinburgh
Printed in the U.S.A. by
Versa Press, Inc.,
East Peoria, IL

CONTENTS

CONTRIBUTORS

The Rev. Dr PETER E. BARNES is the minister of Revesby Presbyterian Church, Sydney, and lectures in Church History at the Presbyterian Theological Centre, Sydney. He contributed Chapters 1 and 4.

The Rev. Dr ANTHONY E. BIRD is lecturer in New Testament Studies at the Presbyterian Theological College, Melbourne. He contributed Chapter 13.

The Rev. BRUCE H. CHRISTIAN is the minister of Rose Bay Presbyterian Church, Sydney. He contributed Chapter 10.

The Rev. ANDREW M. CLARKE is the minister of Bendigo Presbyterian Church, Victoria, and was at the time of original publication Convener of the Church and Nation Committees of the Presbyterian Church of Victoria and the Presbyterian Church of Australia. He contributed the Introduction and Chapter 7.

The Rev. Dr JOHN A. DAVIES is principal of the Presbyterian Theological Centre, Sydney, and lectures in Old Testament and Hebrew. He contributed Chapters 3 and 5.

The Rev. DONALD W. ELLIOTT is the minister of Eltham Presbyterian Church, Melbourne, and lectures part-time in Pastoral Counselling at the Presbyterian Theological College, Melbourne. He contributed the chapter summaries, 'The Bottom Line'.

The Rev. Dr GREGORY R. GOSWELL is lecturer in Old Testament Studies at the Presbyterian Theological College, Melbourne. He contributed Chapter 8.

The Rev. Dr ALLAN M. HARMAN is research professor at the Presbyterian Theological College, Melbourne. He contributed Chapters 6 and 14.

The Rev. JARED C. HOOD is the minister of Moe Presbyterian Church, Victoria, and lectures part-time in Biblical Studies at the Presbyterian Theological College, Melbourne. He contributed Chapter 12.

The Rev. Dr DOUGLAS J. W. MILNE is principal of the Presbyterian Theological College, Melbourne, and lectures in Theology and Ethics. He contributed Chapters 2, 9 and 15, and the Study Guide.

The Rev. BARRY R. OAKES is the minister of Noorat Presbyterian Church, Victoria. He contributed Chapter 11.

PUBLISHER'S NOTE

The Church and Nation Committee of the Presbyterian Church of Victoria, Australia, first published LOVE RULES in 2004. Its short but weighty chapters on each of the Ten Commandments, together with introductory and concluding material and a valuable Study Guide, are intended to help combat the widespread ignorance of the Commandments which prevails today, and to help Christians and non-Christians alike to see the importance of the law of God for all of life.

But the underlying reason for writing a book about the law, as the introduction affirms, is for the sake of the gospel. It is impossible, the contributors believe, to preach the genuine gospel without the law. 'By the law is the knowledge of sin' (*Rom.* 3:20, KJV), and without this knowledge the gospel will seem an idle tale. For the sake of man's life in this world *and* in the world to come, therefore, there are few things more urgently needed today than an understanding of the moral law summarized in the Ten Commandments.

The present publisher sends out this introduction to the Ten Commandments with the prayer that God may be pleased to use it to increase the knowledge of both law and gospel, to the glory of his own holy name.

THE PUBLISHER
April 2007

INTRODUCTION

Q. *Why write a book on the law?*
A. *Because of the gospel.*

Jesus commenced his preaching ministry with the call: 'Repent, and believe in the gospel' (*Mark* 1:15). Repent of what? Is there a clear moral standard in the Bible that reveals the holiness of God, the sinfulness of man, and the purity of new life in Christ? Yes, there is.

The place of the moral law in relation to the gospel has become one of the most controversial issues for the evangelical church today. The Ten Commandments are rarely asserted with confidence, and generally minimized with embarrassment. Their thorough and diverse application in the Scriptures is conspicuously absent in discipleship and worship, resulting in 'repentance' without content and authenticity.

The end result is that less than 1 per cent of church members can list the Ten Commandments. The liberal illusion of 'I am a good person' persists, and a younger generation of 'new liberals' believe that they can identify with Jesus without serious interest in the extent of his claims upon them. The latter professing evangelicals believe themselves to represent 'true Christianity' as much as the former liberals.

Previous generations of evangelicals taught their children to memorize the Ten Commandments before they turned their attention to John 3:16. Why? Because they believed that any understanding of John 3:16 would be grossly deficient without a prior knowledge of the moral law. Charles Spurgeon compared the law to the needle that draws after it the silk thread of the gospel.

The clear pattern of evangelistic preaching in the New Testament is that of God's holiness, man's sinfulness, Christ's glory, and the call to repentance and faith. When missionary John Eliot went to the American Indians, and John Paton to the New Hebrides, what was the first thing they preached? The Ten Commandments, as was typical of their age. It is sadly true that in our day some preach the law without the gospel. Some preach neither the law nor the gospel. However, no matter how hard one tries, one cannot genuinely preach the gospel without the law.

The Ten Commandments are commonly feared to be all about deprivation. However, our Saviour, in calling us to repentance in terms of the moral law, purposes to deprive us only of sin and its consequences, and to reconcile us to God through union with himself, whom to know is life in all its fullness. There can be no doubt that, in the confusion about the Ten Commandments, a biblical understanding of justification and sanctification has been the most tragic casualty.

We are very grateful to our contributors and those who have assisted in the preparation of this book. We offer it to you as an evangelistic and discipleship tool. It is a contemporary introduction to, and theological and ethical explanation of, the Ten Commandments. No attempt is made to answer every question. We aim to point our readers in the historic

Introduction

Reformed direction (consistent with the Westminster Standards) and to get them thinking. Let the dialogue begin!

We pray that this small volume might be used of God in awakening zeal for his glory, inspiring faithful preaching, encouraging wise living, and initiating true revival throughout our churches.

ANDREW CLARKE
Presbyterian Church of Victoria,
Australia

I

DO WE NEED THE TEN COMMANDMENTS IN THE TWENTY-FIRST-CENTURY CHURCH AND WORLD?

THE MODERN SITUATION

Why should we cling to what some escaped slaves, resting from the desert sun at Mount Sinai, thought their tribal deity said to them, back in the dark days before there was television? Indeed, how do we even know that it happened at all? There were no cameras there to record the event.

Why should we be any more inclined to follow the dictates of the Bible than those of the texts of Qumran or Nag Hammadi, texts that very nearly perished through being eaten by a goat or by being used as fuel to warm a camel driver's household?

There is no doubt that, for the most part, the western world has discarded the notion of the need for obedience to God's law, as summarized in the Ten Commandments. As the Australian Parliament discussed the issue of embryonic stem cell research in 2001, Senator Amanda Vanstone claimed that religion had no place in the debate. Such a view conveniently sidelines all Christians from the political arena, leaving it free only for the humanists. In the U.S.A. a Federal Court ruled that reciting the pledge, with its words, 'One nation under God', is unconstitutional.

In the original Hebrew, the Ten Commandments are given to us in only one hundred and seventy-three words, whereas we are told there are almost 30,000 words in the European Union's regulations on the importation of cauliflowers. Having departed from God's law, the West has entered the age of lawyers. It has proved less than edifying. As Tacitus remarked, 'The more corrupt the state, the more numerous the laws.'

The modern secular state wants people to be compassionate, tolerant, honest, and caring, but has great difficulty in defining these terms and motivating its subjects to embrace them. Law makes little sense and carries little real authority without a lawgiver. The result is ludicrous. We mock God as lawgiver, but still hope that people will behave themselves.

We are now left with a vague desire to do the right thing and not be anti-social. Often there are claims that we should be morally neutral, but these are highly selective. One rarely hears the claim that we ought to be morally neutral over racism or paedophilia. Ultimately, moral neutrality is no position. The western world is afflicted with increasing sin, but a decreasing sense of sin. We have returned to the creed of Rousseau, 'Whatever I feel to be right is right. Whatever I feel to be wrong is wrong.' Such is the condition of humanity, without a revelation from God.

THREEFOLD USE OF THE LAW

Evangelical theology has traditionally been able to see connections between law (God's holy demands) and grace

(God's free promises). The law is binding (*Matt.* 5:17–20; *Rom.* 3:31; *Jer.* 31:33), yet there is a sense in which the Christian is released from the law (*Rom.* 6:14; 7:1–6; *2 Cor.* 3:11; *Gal.* 3:25; 5:18). Although some claim that the Bible does not divide the law into moral, ceremonial, and civil elements, it is difficult to see how the various strands of Scripture can be reconciled unless such a distinction is maintained.

The law is never separated from God's love but flows from it (*Deut.* 33:2–3). Christ fulfilled the law, which effectively abolished the ceremonial part of it (*Heb.* 5–10). It is true that the law is unified (*James* 2:8–11), but here James is referring to the abiding relevance of the moral law. In short, law makes grace necessary, and grace confirms law (*Psa.* 40:8; 119:97; *John* 15:10; *1 John* 2:3–5; 3:21–22; 5:3).

According to John Flavel the Puritan, 'There is a good and an evil use of the law.' We read the same thing in Paul, 'Now we know that the law is good, if one uses it lawfully' (*1 Tim.* 1:8). The sixteenth-century Reformers, more particularly John Calvin, discerned three major uses of the law:

To convict the sinner of sin. Paul declared that the law did not acquit any sinner before God, but by the law came the knowledge of sin (*Rom.* 3:20). In Paul's own case, it was especially the tenth commandment, which forbids coveting (*Rom.* 7:7). The law is no man's saviour, but it shows us that we need to be saved.

C. S. Lewis recalled that when he first came to university, he was as nearly without a moral conscience as a boy could be. Such a person sees no need of Christ as Redeemer until the Spirit convicts him of sin, righteousness, and judgment (*John* 16:8–11). The Spirit does this partly by revealing the full depth of God's holy law (*Matt.* 5–7).

To restrain evil. To use Samuel Bolton's graphic image, the law chains the wolf, while the gospel changes him. The law does not make us good but usually, albeit not always (*Rom.* 7:8–9), acts to curb our sinful instincts. We are 'held captive under the law' (*Gal.* 3:23). If a man does not burgle my house because of the law against stealing, that hardly makes him a new creation in Christ, but it does mean my house is not burgled. Sin is not eradicated, but the expression of it is restrained. To cite Calvin: 'This constrained and forced righteousness is necessary to the community of men, for the tranquillity which our Saviour provides by preventing all things from being overturned in confusion, which is what would happen if everything were permitted to everyone.'

To guide the Christian. Love fulfils the law; it does not abolish it (*Rom.* 13:8–10). The Christian is under the law of Christ (*1 Cor.* 9:21; *Gal.* 6:2). Those who abolish this third use of the law have difficulty in defining clearly how the Christian should live, and how the moral law reflects the unchanging holy character of God. Thomas Watson considered this most serious indeed: 'They who will not have the law to rule them, shall never have the gospel to save them.'

THE PRESENT NEED

There are challenges from all sides today to the authority and relevance of the Ten Commandments. Modern secular society is determined to make up its own ethics, with the over-riding virtue being, not love, but tolerance. Meanwhile a retreating church is often fearful of offending the world at large. In seeking to avoid legalism (trying to keep the law in order to be saved), we flee to antinomianism (discarding God's law) and then construct a new legalism (we make up our own set of regulations). Hence intolerance and sexism are treated as sins in the modern world. Even in evangelical circles, matters are not made as clear as they should be. The law of Moses does not provide a complete and binding guide to Christian morality. On the other hand it should not be dismissed as irrelevant.

The approach adopted by situation ethics (where we decide what is right by the circumstances) abolishes law. Joseph Fletcher says, 'Only love is a constant; everything else is a variable.' To which we might add the claims of Paul Tillich, 'The law of love is the ultimate law because it is the negation of law.' This approach has a tendency to be translated into the somewhat simple 1960s philosophy of Jerry Rubin: 'If it feels good, do it.' The Bible's reply to this would be that the heart is deceitful above all things (*Jer.* 17:9), and the language of love can easily be used to disguise deep-seated selfishness and immorality (note the example of Amnon in *2 Sam.* 13:1–15).

We are no better off if we try to make the law stand on its own. Motive is important in what we do (*Matt.* 6:1; *Mark* 12:43–44). So too is context; those who are going to misuse the truth, for example, have no right to hear it (*Exod.* 1; *Josh.* 2; *1 Sam.* 16:2). The Christian is purified as he maintains his hope of seeing Christ in glory (*1 John* 3:2–3). Law is vital but it is not to be treated in isolation. Bonhoeffer put forward the biblical view: 'There can be no preaching of the law without the gospel, and no preaching of the gospel without the law.' Law needs to be distinguished from grace and love, but to separate these three is to rend asunder what God has joined.

PETER BARNES

THE BOTTOM LINE

• The Ten Commandments provide a reference point for morality outside of human opinions.

• The Ten Commandments help provide greater definition to the meaning of love and to what Jesus called the two greatest commandments (*Matt.* 22:36–40).

• The Ten Commandments also expose our human flaws (*Rom.* 3:19–20), point us to Christ (*John* 5:24; *Rom.* 3:21) and to our need for redemption (*Rom.* 3:21–25).

2

THE RELATIONSHIP BETWEEN LAW AND LOVE

Behind the debate about the relationship between law and love lies a deeper one about the relationship between the Old Testament and the New Testament. Those who see little or no continuity between the two will favour love over law; those who believe real continuity exists between the two will emphasize law as well as love. Historically Lutherans and Dispensationalists have taken the first position, whereas the Reformed churches have taken the second.

LAW

Within the New Testament 'law' has a range of meanings such as 'the Scriptures' (*1 Cor.* 14:34), 'a principle of activity' (*Rom.* 3:27), 'God's covenant with Israel' (*Gal.* 3:17), 'a body of divine regulations' (*Eph.* 2:15), or 'the moral commandments' (*Rom.* 7:12). In this chapter we are interested in law in the last sense. The New Testament clearly teaches the function of the law in awakening people to a personal and radical knowledge of sin (*Rom.* 3:20; 5:20; 7:7–12; *Gal.* 3:19; *1 Tim.* 1:9). The question is whether the moral law also serves as a guide in living the Christian life. In trying to answer this question there are four facts we may recognize.

The moral law reflects what God is like. When Paul describes the moral law as being holy, righteous, and good (*Rom.* 7:12) or glorious (*2 Cor.* 3:7–9), he is applying attributes of God to his law. The moral law is a mirror of God's own being and is therefore as complete as the character of God.

The moral law is part of creation. In Genesis 2:2–3 God appoints the Sabbath day as an institution of his creation covenant. When he makes his salvation covenant with Israel, creation is the reason for the fourth commandment (*Exod.* 20:8–11). The oracles against the nations in the major prophets of Israel are further proof of a permanent moral order in the world (*Isa.* 13–24; *Jer.* 46–50; *Ezek.* 25–32; *Amos* 1–2). This is in full agreement with Paul's teaching that the work of God's moral law is written on men's hearts so that they sometimes naturally do what the law requires (*Rom.* 2:14–15). Jesus teaches that his kingdom restores the creation order in moral questions. He cites the example of marriage and divorce in Matthew 19:3–6. The gospel therefore upholds and restores the moral law of creation.

The moral law is the heart of Israel's covenant law. Sometimes the objection is made that the Bible does not differentiate Old Testament law into its ceremonial, civil, and moral parts. But the moral law summed up in the Ten Commandments was from the beginning singled out as being the heart of God's covenant. This appears from a number of facts:

• only the Ten Commandments were written on the tablets of stone (*Exod.* 34:27–28);

• these tablets of the Ten Commandments were inserted into the ark of the covenant below the mercy seat (*Heb.* 9: 3–5);

• the covenant was known as the covenant of the ten words (*Exod.* 34:28; *Deut.* 4:13). The moral law therefore takes precedence over other parts of the Mosaic covenant.

The moral law is part of the gospel. Jesus (*Matt.* 5:17–32) defends the permanent authority of the moral law by saying that he has come to 'fulfil' it (5:17). In the rest of chapter 5 he shows what this means by filling out its application to the whole of life in the radical demands of kingdom morality. Creation will pass away before the moral teaching of the Old Testament does (5:18). Greatness in the kingdom of heaven means teaching and living out the commands of God (5:19). Kingdom righteousness means excelling that of the scribes and Pharisees that consists merely in external forms (5:20).

THE ROLE OF THE SPIRIT

In Romans 8:1–4, Paul argues that the Spirit of Christ enables believers to fulfil the moral norms of God's law. In 1 Corinthians 7:19 Paul claims that moral obedience to God's commandments is more important than receiving the sign of circumcision. In 1 Corinthians 9:21 the apostle defines his relationship to law by stating that he does not live outside God's law but within Christ's law. This suggests that he has made a synthesis of the moral law of the Old Testament and Christ's new law of love (*Gal.* 6:2). In Ephesians 6:2–3 he explicitly cites the words of the fifth commandment as a basis for understanding what being a Christian child means in practice.

THE PLACE OF CONSCIENCE

Finally, we ought not to overlook the place of conscience in the Christian life. Conscience functions in conjunction with God's moral law (*Rom.* 2:14–15). Paul repeatedly appeals to his conscience to attest the integrity of his Christian life, and warns against its neglect in practice (*Acts* 24:16; *Rom.* 9:1; *2 Cor.* 4:2; *1 Tim.* 1:5, 18–19).

LOVE

The New Testament gives a special prominence to love in its moral teaching because God has displayed his love in a special way in the gospel. Jesus initiates this emphasis (*John* 13:34–35), followed by Paul (*1 Cor.* 13), then the rest of the New Testament writers (*Heb.* 13:1; *James* 2:8; *1 Pet.* 4:8; *2 Pet.* 1:5–7; *1 John* 4:7–8). In particular, Jesus summed up the whole of biblical morality in terms of an integrated love: to God with our whole being, and to our neighbour as ourselves (*Matt.* 22:36–40).

1 Corinthians 13 is the classic teaching on love, but Christian love goes back to God's Trinitarian love in the gospel. We learn what love means from what God has done for us in giving up his Son for us all (*Rom.* 5:6–8). God's love in Christ is a servant love that acts sacrificially to secure the good of others who do not deserve that love (*Phil.* 2:5–8). The Holy Spirit witnesses to that love in the Christian's heart and constrains us to a life of love in return (*Rom.* 5:5; 8:2–4; *Gal.* 5:22–23).

Love is an attitude of goodwill towards the other person that not only aims but acts to benefit that other without counting the cost. Love is creative and outgoing. Love is the key to fruitful and peaceful relationships. Love lies at the heart of Christian morality. This is because love is at the heart of God (*1 John* 4:8, 16).

LAW AND LOVE

In several places the New Testament unites law and love in a reciprocal way. In Romans 13:8–10 and in Galatians 5:13–14, Paul holds love as the fulfilling of God's moral law. By this he does not mean that the moral commands are redundant in the presence of love. Rather, he means that without love, morality is formal and lifeless, a parody of what goodness, truth, and justice ought to be.

According to James 2:8–13 love transforms our experience of law-keeping into freedom. But Christian freedom is about being freed from sin so as to serve our neighbour in love (*Gal.* 5:13). God's moral law is like a charter of my neighbour's rights, and love leads me to respect them in practice.

The need for law along with love is clear from the nature of both. Law is prescriptive, love is motivational; law is propositional, love is dispositional; law is like a road-map, love is like a compass. The road-map indicates the way to get to our destination; love sets us in the right direction. Both are needed but each helps us in a different way.

Law without love results in coldness and often masks double standards; love without law results in false freedom and often masks the proud spirit of an imagined superior spirituality. Together, law and love form the standard of Christ-like example for every believer. The Christian loves God's law (*Psa.* 119:97; *Rom.* 7:22) because God has inscribed it on his heart, just as he promised (*Jer.* 31:33; *2 Cor.* 3).

CONCLUSIONS

Theologically, God is light as well as love (*1 John* 1:5; 4:8, 16). For this reason he calls us to practise both moral righteousness and Christian love in serving him.

Hermeneutically, moral commandments are not the whole of ethical wisdom. New Testament writers appeal to other supplementary sources of moral wisdom such as nature (*1 Cor.* 11:14), Christ's example (*Phil.* 2:5–8), church tradition (*1 Cor.* 14:33–34), the gospel (*1 Cor.* 6:14–15) and experience (*2 Tim.* 2:20–21).

Historically, Reformed theology might have been better, following Augustine, to have made the love commandments of Jesus its starting-point when interpreting the moral law (*Matt.* 22:37–40).

Practically, we are to aim at love in all our Christian obedience and to keep on working at love (*1 Cor.* 13; *Phil.* 1:9–11). We always owe a debt of love (*Rom.* 13:8).

Ecclesiastically, we need to be building communities of love in our congregations, as a living witness to the truth of Christianity (*John* 13:34–35; *1 Thess.* 4:9–10; *1 Pet.* 4:8).

Douglas Milne

THE BOTTOM LINE

• The moral law reflects the unchanging character of God and his intentions for those made in his image.

• The moral law is built into the creation order and is highlighted in the Mosaic Covenant, rather than being a unique part of that Old Testament Covenant.

• Because the moral law flows from the goodness and love of God, we are to value it as necessary for peace and harmony in all our relationships.

• Law and love go together. Love keeps us from coldness and double standards; law keeps us from false freedom and pride.

3

THE INTRODUCTION TO THE TEN COMMANDMENTS

And God spoke all these words, saying, 'I am the Lord
your God, who brought you out of the land of Egypt,
out of the house of slavery' (Exod. 20:1–2).

THE IMPORTANCE OF CONTEXT

Readers of the Bible could well adopt the real estate agent's slogan: 'Location, location, location'. Or to use the word Bible students generally use, CONTEXT is vital for understanding any passage. Too often, the Ten Commandments have been learned, recited, displayed on church walls, and disparaged, all without reference to the surrounding framework of Scripture in which they are set. Divorced from their context, they become simply a set of timeless moral principles, the standard to which all must aspire if we are to be in God's good books, as though keeping them were well within the grasp of people of good will.

Then again, the Ten Commandments are sometimes treated with only half an eye on their context. They are part of the Old Testament, a body of literature, it is felt, which reflects God's experiment with human obedience as a means of achieving salvation, an experiment which was doomed to dismal failure. Now, it is sometimes said, we have moved on to an era of grace where law has been dealt a crushing blow as the enemy of the gospel. Its only lingering function is to remind us how fortunate we are to have moved on to better things.

There are glimmers of truth in each of the above sentiments, but only glimmers. For too long, we have failed to give sufficient weight to the biblical contexts (for there are two) in which the Ten Commandments are set out, and, as a result, we have failed to grasp their full significance. As with any document we read, we need to ask: Who is it addressed to, and, What is its purpose? To answer these questions, we will consider the prologue to the commandments, and its wider setting in the book of Exodus.

The opening verses of Exodus 20 provide us with the key to our understanding of who the Ten Commandments are for, and why they are given:

And God spoke all these words, saying, 'I am the LORD your God, who brought you out of the land of Egypt, out of the house of slavery' (*Exod.* 20:1–2).

These words tell us:

- that the speaker is none other than God himself.

- that the people addressed are in a special relationship with God.

- that the relationship is one based on God's powerful and gracious deliverance of this people from slavery.

THE GOD WHO SPEAKS

It has often been felt that the account of the Ten Command-ments is somehow out of place in the book of Exodus. Would it not have made more sense to wait until Moses ascended the mountain to receive the stone tablets on which they are engraved (24:12–31:18) before recounting the com-mandments?

Chapter 20 follows directly on the dramatic manifestation of God (accompanied by thunder and lightning, thick cloud, smoke and earthquake) in chapter 19. By having God speak the words directly in the hearing of all Israel at this point in the narrative, the writer gives the reader who does not directly experience the dramatic events a sense of the awe-some character of God, and the authority inherent in the words. It is this character which explains why access to God's presence will not come cheaply; hence the elaborate precau-tions lest anyone should touch the mountain.

The God who speaks is identified as the LORD, the name by which he revealed himself to Moses in the burning bush (*Exod.* 3:14–15). The meaning of this name might be rendered as 'the One who is sovereignly present (with his people)'. This God reveals himself as the God who tolerates no rivals, the God of all history, the God who made all that there is.

This God is a relational God, who made people to enjoy his world in companionship with himself. The rebellion with which God was confronted in the garden of Eden was not to have the last word, as God embarked on a long-range plan to restore the world he had pronounced *good,* and once more to live in the midst of his people.

THE PEOPLE ADDRESSED

The Ten Commandments are addressed to a people who have come to enjoy a uniquely privileged relationship with God ('your God'). This calls to mind the commitment God had made to their ancestors, Abraham, Isaac and Jacob, a commitment that he would be with them, that he would be their God. At Mount Sinai, the presence of God promised to the patriarchs, and foreshadowed in the encounter with Moses in Exodus 3, becomes the experience of the whole people.

Upon their arrival at Sinai, God makes an incredible commitment to his people, promising them: 'Now therefore, if you will indeed obey my voice and keep my covenant, you shall be my treasured possession among all peoples, for all the earth is mine; and you shall be to me a kingdom of priests and a holy nation. These are the words that you shall speak to the people of Israel' (*Exod.* 19:5–6).

The word for 'treasured possession' is a relational word of the highest order. It speaks of that which is most cherished, and was particularly applied, in the language of diplomacy, by a greater king to a lesser king whom he regarded as his most loyal and trusted ally and friend. The word is unpacked as meaning that Israel is to be uniquely for God 'a kingdom of priests and a holy nation' (see also *1 Pet.* 2:5, 9; *Rev.* 1:6; 5:10; 20:6). God's people are the honoured guests he loves to have in his presence, a truth illustrated in the banquet enjoyed by the people's representatives in the divine palace (*Exod.* 24:9–11).

There can be no higher honour than to attend upon this God in joyful service. God's people are a holy people; that is, they reflect the character of God himself, for without this compatibility with the character of God, no-one will experience a relationship with him (*Heb.* 12:14).

What then, is the force of the words, 'If you will indeed obey my voice and keep my covenant' (*Exod.* 19:5)? While keeping God's law has often been treated as an impossibility, the whole thrust of the passage is that what God is promising is a gracious reality. It is as Israel submits to God's requirements that they experience the reality of the privileged relationship. The commandments will simply fill out something of what it means to enjoy God.

THE SPECIAL RELATIONSHIP
BETWEEN GOD AND ISRAEL

As recounted in Exodus 1-18, the relationship God has with Israel is one characterized by his sovereign, gracious, and powerful act of redemption. In keeping with his commitment to Abraham, when the people of Israel found themselves in Egypt, serving a different king, the King of the universe set about to demonstrate who was really in control. The plagues which devastated the land of Egypt were a commentary on the supremacy of the true God over the false gods of the Egyptians. The final deliverance of the enslaved people came in the form of an echo of the original creation, where water and dry land were separated, enabling the people of Israel to cross the Red Sea in safety to freedom. 'You have led in your steadfast love the people whom you have redeemed; you have guided them by your strength to your holy abode' (*Exod.* 15:13).

There can be no suggestion that the commandments are given as a means to securing salvation, or a relationship with God. Rather, they spell out the character of a relationship which is already there by divine favour. They encapsulate the character of God and his design for His people's life in the land, in fellowship with him and with one another. These are the gracious laws particularly intended for a redeemed people, but they are binding for all humanity.

TODAY

How then do the words of the prologue to the commandments relate to us today? The answer to this question may help us to understand the way in which the commandments themselves relate to us. Christian believers are heirs to the promises made to Abraham (*Rom.* 4:16), and to Israel at Mount Sinai (*1 Pet.* 2:9). We are those who have been redeemed, not by crossing a body of water, but by the death and resurrection of Jesus Christ, through which we cross from death to life (*Rom.* 3:24; *Eph.* 1:7; 2:1–10; *Col.* 1:14; *Heb.* 9:12). Christ has accomplished his 'exodus' (*Luke* 9:31) on our behalf. We are free from bondage, not to Egyptian task-masters, but to a more powerful adversary (*Rom.* 6:22; *Rev.* 1:5). Those who are in Christ are a holy people (*1 Cor.* 3:7; *Eph.* 1:4; *Col.* 3:12; *1 Pet.* 1:2), fit for access to God's presence. This is our true place of residence (*Eph.* 2:6).

The history of the people of God in the Old Testament becomes our history, its promises our promises, and the character of the God of Israel is the character of the God who reveals himself supremely in Jesus. While this may not directly answer the question of the manner in which the commandments address us today, it will mean that the question cannot be avoided as irrelevant. We are those who, like Israel at Sinai, enjoy an intimate relationship with the holy God who has rescued us from slavery and brought us into fellowship with himself. We, too, would do well, then, to listen to God's voice from the mountain and to respond in love and trust.

JOHN DAVIES

THE BOTTOM LINE

• The God who gives guidance and direction for right living is first and foremost a redeeming God of mercy.

• Redeemed people in particular are called to live according to God's standards.

• It should be a joy and pleasure to acknowledge God for who he is and reflect his character in all our relationships.

4

THE FIRST COMMANDMENT

You shall have no other gods before me (Exod. 20:3).

THE 'CHALLENGE' TO GOD

The Bible does not spend much time arguing for the existence of God. It dismisses as a fool the one who says in his heart that there is no God (*Psa.* 14:1). One is without excuse if one cannot discern from the creation that there is an all-powerful Creator (*Rom.* 1:20).

All rival gods are not gods at all (*Psa.* 96:5; *Isa.* 45:21; 46: 1–2; *Jer.* 14:22). The gods of the Egyptians were not gods at all. Neither were the gods of Ammon, Edom, Moab, Assyria, and Babylon. The gods of Hinduism do not exist, and neither do the gods of Buddhism (if it is claimed that there are any). Even Allah (the God of Islam) and Jehovah (as understood by modern day Judaism) cannot be viewed as the same God as the God of the Bible. The God of modern Christendom, a kindly and tolerant figure who saves all who are sincere, is likewise an idol which cannot be reconciled with the God who has made himself known in the Bible.

Humanism too is a false religion. The second Humanist Manifesto of 1973, issued forty years after the publication of the first one, declares: 'No deity will save us; we must save ourselves.' From the Bible's perspective, and that of common sense, such an assertion is a programme for folly and despair.

The modern mind is reluctant to think in terms of either/or, but the Bible does. Whether it is Joshua at Shechem or Elijah at Mount Carmel, the message is the same. There can be no limping between two opinions: either the Lord is the true God and alone is to be worshipped or he is not, and can be set aside (*Josh.* 24:1, 14–15; *1 Kings* 18:20–21). Any attempt to mix up the worship of the true God with the worship of other gods is always repudiated (*1 Kings* 11:1–11; *2 Kings* 17:33).

The Roman Empire persecuted the early Christians because they said that Jesus is not *a* lord but *the only* Lord. We are fast returning to the same kind of worldview. On 21 August 2001, the editorial of the *Sydney Morning Herald* newspaper pontificated: 'In the multicultural, multigod nation that modern Australia is, proselytising can only needlessly provoke community tensions.'

The modern world, like Rome of old, revels in what it celebrates as spiritual diversity. This approach can be seen in any number of examples. If he becomes king, Prince Charles wishes to be 'Defender of Faith' (i.e., Defender of All Faiths), not 'Defender of the Faith'. After the Port Arthur Massacre in April 1996 there was an Inter-Faith service in the Anglican Cathedral in Hobart to mourn the dead. In 1986, and again in 2002 at Assisi (associated with St Francis of Assisi), Pope John Paul II worshipped with Muslims, Hindus, the Dali Lama, and assorted Shamans, and prayed for world peace. Mahatma Gandhi once declared: 'I am a Christian and a Hindu and a Moslem and a Jew.' He used to say, 'The soul of all religions is one.'

In 1993 the Board of World Mission and Unity of the Church of Scotland informed the General Assembly that Christians ought to 'seek to discern the activity of the Word in other faiths, as well as in the world today'. Sincere believers in other faiths might well be acceptable to God, so the Board said. The Rev. Ian Hamilton of Newmilns, Ayrshire, moved that the Assembly reaffirm that Jesus Christ is the only Saviour of men and women, only to see his motion defeated by about 400 votes to 300.

The Bible, on the other hand, declares that there is but one Saviour (*Isa.* 43:11). There is but one mediator between God and men (*1 Tim.* 2:5), one way to the Father in heaven (*John* 14:6) and one name which saves (*Acts* 4:12). God alone is to be worshipped, as he has made himself known in Jesus Christ. In the New Testament, Jesus Christ claims the same allegiance that was due to the LORD in the Old Testament (*Luke* 14:26).

NO OTHER GODS

The first commandment declares, 'You shall have no other gods before me' (*Exod.* 20:3; *Deut.* 5:7). Other gods are an ever-present danger, then as now. On 23 January 1945 Helmuth James, Count von Moltke (a Protestant member of the Kreisau Circle, a discussion group which made plans for Germany after what it saw as the inevitable defeat of the Nazis), was hanged on the orders of Friesler, the President of the People's Court. During one of his tirades, Friesler told the Count: 'We and Christianity resemble each other in only one respect: we claim the whole man!' Abraham had come from Mesopotamia where there was a multitude of gods (*Josh.* 24:1–2). Presumably at Ur, Abraham knew of and perhaps had participated in the worship of the moon god, which possessed the appropriate name of Sin! Moses and the Israelites had known at first hand the gods of Egypt, which included the sun, the crocodile, the scarab beetle, the Nile River, and Pharaoh himself. Canaan may have been a land flowing with milk and honey, but it also overflowed with gods, such as the fertility god Baal, his female consort Asherah, and Moloch, whose worship demanded child sacrifice.

There are good reasons, both historical and philosophical, why the Ten Commandments are headed by the Lord's call for unswerving allegiance to him first of all. In the words of the Puritan, Thomas Watson, 'This may well lead the van, and be set in the front of all the commandments, because it is the foundation of all true religion.' John Calvin too has commented: 'Surely the first foundation of righteousness is the worship of God. When this is overthrown, all the remaining parts of righteousness, like the pieces of a shattered and fallen building, are mangled and scattered.' Righteousness means nothing unless there is one who has righteousness, indeed who is righteous. We must know God in order to know how to live.

This commandment affirms that there are no other gods, either 'in addition to me' (Keil and Delitzsch), or 'in opposition to me'. More literally, Israel was to have no other gods 'to my face'. God was not simply saying that he is the first God to be worshipped ('no other gods before me') but the *only* God to be worshipped ('no other gods besides me'). In a world of polytheism, Israel was called to serve the one true God, the Creator of the world, the Judge of the world at the time of the Flood, and the covenant God of Abraham, Isaac and Jacob.

No matter how the command is translated exactly, the thrust is clear enough. The Bible is exclusive in its claims about there being one true and living God (*Isa.* 45:5–6, 18, 20–21; *1 Cor.* 8:4). Question 46 of the *Westminster Shorter Catechism* asks, 'What is required in the first commandment?' The answer given is, 'The first commandment requires us to know and acknowledge God to be the only true God, and our God; and to worship and glorify him accordingly.' As Jesus responded to Satan, 'You shall worship the Lord your God and him only shall you serve' (*Matt.* 4:10). The history of Israel, recorded in the Old Testament, bears witness to the consequences of God's covenant people seeking after other gods (e.g. *2 Kings* 17:7-12).

LIVING TODAY

Twice the apostle Paul makes the startling claim that covetousness is idolatry (*Eph.* 5:5; *Col.* 3:5). The implications of this need to be worked out. It means that if we spend our time dreaming of sport, worldly success, cars, or sexual fantasies, we are guilty of breaking the tenth commandment, and also the first. Freedom can become a false god, and so too can a concept like world peace. The cult of health and fitness, while good within certain boundaries, can become an idol. Philosophies which promote self-esteem, empowerment, and the realization of our potential are also candidates for idols. To many earnest spirits, the United Nations has become some kind of substitute-deity, abounding in beneficent wisdom. Modern western man, in this twenty-first century, has not removed God, but installed God-substitutes. As D. L. Moody put it: 'Whatever you love more than God is your idol.' The only godly response is that of William Cowper:

LOVE RULES

> The dearest idol I have known,
> Whate'er that idol be,
> Help me to tear it from Thy throne
> And worship only Thee.

We need to know that there is only one God (*James* 2:19), and we need to love this God with all our being (*Matt.* 22:37–38). Idolatry of any kind should provoke us as it did the apostle Paul at Athens (*Acts* 17:16). We cannot compromise here in the name of a false charity or fellowship. We must not drink the cup of the Lord and the cup of demons, nor eat of the Lord's table and the table of demons (*1 Cor.* 10:20–21). Little children, keep yourselves from idols (*1 John* 5:21).

PETER BARNES

THE BOTTOM LINE

• There is only one living God.

• We should be pleased that God cared enough for us to make this clear and therefore spare us from wasting our time on fakes or falling into superstitious bondage and ultimately, eternal judgment.

• We should be wary of our continual tendency to give god-like importance to things around us.

5

THE SECOND COMMANDMENT

You shall not make for yourself a carved image, or any
likeness of anything that is in heaven above, or that is in
the earth beneath, or that is in the water under the earth.
You shall not bow down to them or serve them, for I the
LORD your God am a jealous God, visiting the iniquity of
the fathers on the children to the third and the fourth
generation of those who hate me, but showing steadfast
love to thousands of those who love me and keep my
commandments (Exod. 20:4–6).

THE PROBLEM

'I like to think of God as . . . ' How often have we heard words like these, perhaps even said them ourselves? It is a common desire on the part of human beings, both those in rebellion against God and those who know his grace (since sinful tendencies remain within us), to want to reduce God to an image, something we can get a handle on, something we can mould and manipulate according to our desires. Few of us have statues of God adorning our homes or our places of worship the way devotees of other religions might (though

31

we might admit to an alleged portrait of Jesus hanging on our wall). But have we really taken heed of the warning given in the second commandment? Have we constructed a convenient image of God which robs him of his truly awesome and gracious character?

NO IMAGES OF GOD

Israel was unique among the religious cultures of the ancient world in not having any officially sanctioned physical images of their God. The central area of the Jerusalem temple (and before that the tabernacle or tent-shrine of the wilderness), where a visiting Canaanite or Egyptian might expect to find such an image, to be tended and cared for and even 'fed' by the priests, was empty, apart from a box containing, among other things, the very laws which spelled out the character of this God and the relationships he envisaged that his people should have with him and with one another. In fact the point is made more obvious by the fact that the cherubim, the creatures with wings outstretched above the box, are pictured as though they were holding up God's invisible throne (*1 Sam.* 4:4; *Psa.* 80:1).

This prohibition of all images did not prevent God's people at times lapsing into the temptation to construct a physical expression of him. The very first breach followed immediately after the giving of the law itself, when Aaron led the people into fashioning a golden bull-image (derisively called a 'calf') to symbolize divine strength (*Exod.* 32). We are left in no doubt as to what God thought of this image of himself. But why should such an image be so condemned, if it helps people focus on God, and on an attribute he undoubtedly possesses? The answer must lie in the fact that our God is the true and living God, and as such, his character and attributes are manifold. He is not simply the God of strength, or any other single feature. What an image conveys at one point, it obscures and distorts at another. Can a bull-image represent the holiness or compassion of God? Can a finite object made by human hands represent the infinity of God? Can an image, which is subject to decay, represent the constancy of God in all of his attributes? Israel's prophets enjoyed their satirical portrayals of idols and those who made them (e.g. *Isa.* 44:9–20; *Jer.* 10:1–5).

Though the first and second commandments are closely connected (which has led some to see them as a single command), we should note that the second commandment does not so much condemn the worship of other gods (which was the substance of the first commandment) as condemn the worship of God in ways which do not do full justice to his revealed character. In a commentary on the second commandment, Moses himself reminds the people of Israel that it was not a visible form of God they encountered at Mount Sinai, but an audible voice (*Deut.* 4:12–20). It is the full-orbed content of God's revelation, in which he sets forth his character and his will for his people, that is to inform our worship.

This same passage also helps to clear up what has sometimes been a misunderstanding of the second commandment and confirms the fact that verses 4 and 5 of Exodus 20 are to be read closely together. It is not any physical representation of 'anything that is in heaven above, or that is in the earth beneath, or that is in the water under the earth' for any purpose that is forbidden. God himself gave instructions about the fashioning of a bronze snake (*Num.* 21:8) and about the adornment of the priestly garments with representations of pomegranates (*Exod.* 28:33). Rather, the prohibition relates to the fabrication of an image of God to serve as a focus or substitute for the worship of God, which would not enhance, but impoverish that worship. The subsequent idolization of the bronze snake by the people of Judah (*2 Kings* 18:4) shows that what may have a legitimate purpose in one context may become a distraction or worse, a snare, in another context.

THE TRUE 'IMAGE' OF GOD

Discussion of the second commandment needs to be brought into relation with the fact that God created humanity to be his image or representation on earth (*Gen.* 1:26–27) and hence no other image is needed. Not, of course that humanity is to be the object of worship, but we are to mirror the character of the God who alone is to be worshipped. While the image of God in humanity was seriously marred by the Fall (our collective rebellion against the authority of God), there is one in whom that image is perfectly restored and displayed. In Jesus Christ, God has given us his full and final revelation of himself (*Col.* 1:13–20; *Heb.* 1:1–4).

In Romans 1:20–25, Paul draws attention to the perversion of the image of God to which we are prone. At any point where we fail to be the people God intended (and this failure can be traced back to the historic Fall, as Paul will go on to explain), we rob God of the glory he is due. So, while we may not have thought of it like this, any failure to reflect the character of God in my life, any neglect of my role as a father, for example, will distort my own and other people's perceptions of who God is, the one I am supposed to represent in this and other ways as his image.

The apostle John ends his first letter on a striking note, 'Little children, keep yourselves from idols' (*1 John* 5:21). At first glance, the introduction of idolatry in the last verse, when there has been no mention of it in the rest of the letter, seems odd. John's letter has been concerned with the identity of Jesus as God come in the flesh, the one through whom we are reconciled to God. It is through our fellowship with him, which finds its expression in a life of obedience and love for other Christians, that we have assurance.

John is not suddenly introducing a new topic in his final verse, but encapsulating all that he has said. Any deviation from a full-orbed understanding of who God in Christ is, and any failure to express that in lives of consistent loving service, is a failure of true worship and a decline into an impoverished perception of the Person and work of God's Son. Any time we trim the grandeur of God's accomplishment in Christ, any time we fall short of the expression of God's will for us, any time we put up barriers or rationalize our lack of fellowship with others of God's people, we slip into the sin of idolatry.

THE SECOND COMMANDMENT AND
A POST-MODERN WORLD

In a post-modern age we need to take the warnings against idolatry (worshipping the true God using objects and images) very seriously. When the notion of absolute truth, or absolute norms, seems outmoded, and what counts is what works for me, the thinking and practice of Christians are inevitably affected. Worship has become relativized into what suits us. We seek what we call 'fellowship' for the sake of what we perceive we gain from it, rather than coming together to give expression to our corporate praise of the God of grace, and thereby building up the church. Within one generation sections of the church have largely abandoned the hymns which collectively sought to give balanced expression to the God of the Bible and to the riches of his grace in Christ. We look in vain for the rich diversity of responses to the character and actions of God which mark the Psalms. Our prayers, which are sometimes introduced by, 'Why don't we just pray' (since we can't think of anything better to do right now), resemble a shopping list. Rarely do they give expression to our profound adoration of the God of the Bible, or our wonder at the depth of his love, or the deep humility and shame we feel before him because of our sin, or our longing to be united with him in eternity.

We are not even immune to the temptation to resort to physical images as 'aids to worship'. While the crosses which adorn our Protestant churches are generally empty, one would have to question the wisdom of placing a cross in a position where it might for some become a focal point of their religious reflection. While it might remind us of the crucified Lord, will it speak as eloquently of his resurrection and ascension? Even those so-called pictures of Jesus, while not necessarily intended as objects of worship, might unwittingly purport to reveal something of the character of the Saviour ('Gentle Jesus meek and mild'), and thereby distort the revelation about him contained in the Scripture.

Each of the commandments is in some sense a window on each of the others. To offend in one point is to break them all (*James* 2:10). Thus to adopt a mental image of God which is less than the one he has revealed will inevitably affect the way we relate to God and the way we live in relation to one another.

The second commandment is as relevant for Christians today as it was for Israel cavorting around a golden calf.

JOHN DAVIES

THE BOTTOM LINE

- Making a representation of God in the form of any created image degrades God and reduces our understanding of him.

- We should be thankful that God is so awesome that nothing in all creation is remotely like him.

- We should be wary of the many ways in which we reduce God to something less than what he really is, even by the way we live as bearers of his image.

6

THE THIRD COMMANDMENT

You shall not take the name of the LORD your God in
vain, for the LORD will not hold him guiltless who
takes his name in vain (Exod. 20:7).

THE NEXT ASPECT OF TRUTH

The order in which the commandments appear is important, for they commence with God the Redeemer claiming
exclusive worship from the people he has redeemed. True
worship must not be given through any medium such as
idols. The third commandment follows on to prohibit the
misuse of God's name, with the added warning that God will
not hold guiltless the person who takes his name falsely.

Several of the expressions in this commandment need
comment, before we can set out its significance. Many discus-
sions on it assume that it is about forbidding the use of God's
name when taking false oaths. Hence it is virtually equivalent
to the ninth commandment, 'You shall not bear false witness
against your neighbour.' It would be strange if there were two
commandments bearing on almost the same subject. Also, if
the breach of the third commandment provokes divine punishment, why then is a similar curse missing from the ninth

commandment? Before the meaning of the commandment can be explained, its translation from Hebrew into English has to be considered.

To take. While the verb 'to take' is common in the Old Testament, when it is used in regard to speech, that is made plain by the addition of words like 'on the lips', or 'with my mouth'. Nowhere does it refer to speech when the verb stands alone.

The name of the Lord is an important expression. In general, and specifically in relation to God's 'name', something more is indicated than just the word by which a person or thing is known. When Moses asked the question in relation to the Lord, 'What is his name?', he had in mind the character by which God revealed himself (*Exod.* 3:13). Whatever sin is meant in this commandment, it is related to the 'character' of God.

In the Old Testament, application of a name to a person or place often signified the existence of a relationship of possession. Just as God named the various aspects of creation, so Adam, in imitating him named the animals and so demonstrated his dominion over them (*Gen.* 2:19). To give a name to a conquered city (*2 Sam.* 12:28) or to lands (*Psa.* 49:11) signified the right of possession.

Putting these factors together suggests that bearing the name of God is not so much speaking about God or using his name in a particular way as bearing the character of God. The Israelites were to demonstrate to the world that they were a people called by the name of the Lord (*Deut.* 28:10). Another helpful parallel occurs in Numbers 6:27 where the Lord says that his name will be put on the people of Israel in the priestly blessing. This is the positive statement corresponding to the negative one in the third commandment.

In vain. The phrase in the commandment often translated 'in vain' has a far wider meaning than this English expression suggests. It is used of things that have no reality to them (like idols), or worthless offerings that are without substance (*Isa.* 1:13). In many contexts, our English word 'hypocritically' fits the situation best.

On the basis of these factors the translation of the commandment could be: 'You must not bear the character of God hypocritically.' In other words, the command to the covenant people was that they, upon whom the Lord had set his name, were not to live in an unreal way. True commitment to him had to be based on reality. There was no place for sham or hypocrisy in his service. Anyone who was called by the name of the LORD, and was a bearer of his character, had to reflect the reality of the living God in their lives.

The commandment does not just give a negative command. Appended to it is a clause that is intended to impress on Israel the need to obey the positive injunction: 'For the LORD will not hold him guiltless who takes his name hypocritically'. Clauses such as this appear often in the Old Testament, reinforcing the importance of a particular command or issuing a warning that will apply if the command is breached. The word 'guiltless' means free from punishment. It is used of exemption from military service (*Deut.* 24:5), or of a husband's freedom from iniquity if, when declaring his wife unfaithful, he followed the legal procedures (*Num.* 5:31). Being held guiltless is the opposite of bearing iniquity. In Exodus 34, as the covenant is renewed after the people sinned while Moses was still on Mount Sinai, God declares his own character (34:6–7) in words taken largely from the second and third commandments: 'The LORD, the LORD, a God merciful and gracious, slow to anger, and abounding in steadfast love and faithfulness, keeping steadfast love for thousands, forgiving iniquity and transgression and sin, but who will by no means clear the guilty . . .'

The contrast is clear. While God by nature is abundant in covenant love and faithfulness, yet he is at the same time the God who will not permit the transgressor to go unpunished.

The motive for obeying this commandment is not an isolated expression of a curse against a transgressor. In common with the extra-biblical treaties, the Old Testament covenants embody blessings and curses. They occur in summary fashion in the Decalogue but are spelled out far more fully in Leviticus 26 and Deuteronomy 27–28.

Here in the third commandment is a divine curse. The threat is that anyone of the holy nation who failed to live in the pattern set for them, will be regarded as guilty before God. The covenant people had a responsibility to imitate their God and so to display his character to the world. This practical display was for a missionary purpose, as Israel would attract others to a similar commitment to the living God.

The understanding of the third commandment set out above means that the sin spoken about does not just relate to speech, but rather something at the very core of life in the covenant. This interpretation is not new, for in the history of Christian thought many have suggested that the commandment has an application that goes far beyond the matter of speech. This is shown by the way in which the Westminster divines dealt with the breadth of this sin (see *Westminster Shorter Catechism,* Questions 54–55, and *Westminster Larger Catechism,* Question 113). In particular the wording in the *Larger Catechism* heads in the right direction when it says that this commandment forbids 'making profession of religion in hypocrisy'. That expression is very apt, and goes to the heart of the prohibition.

Central to the thought of this commandment is the unique position that Israel had in relation to God. He had declared Israel to be his firstborn son (*Exod.* 4:22–23) and had adopted Israel as his own people (*Exod.* 6:7). Part of Israel's role was to be a kingdom of priests and a holy nation (*Exod.* 19:6). That meant that each believing person in Israel had a responsibility to live as part of the special people of God, and bearing the name of God was intrinsic to that role. A false profession of faith in and commitment to the LORD meant repudiation of the covenant bond itself. The third commandment, with its associated curse, served as a reminder to Israel that she needed to fulfil her election and demonstrate the character of God to the world.

The basic idea set out in this commandment finds confirmation in the New Testament, especially in the letters of Paul and Peter. Paul encourages the Ephesians to live in accordance with their new character: the Ephesian Christians were to 'put on the new self, created after the likeness of God in true righteousness and holiness' (*Eph.* 4:24).

Elsewhere Paul calls believing Christians 'God's chosen ones, holy and beloved' (*Col.* 3:12). They are an adopted people who have been made into a royal priesthood and a holy nation, and they are expected to live in such a way that they declare the praises of God. The aim is that pagans may come to glorify God through such Christian witness (*1 Pet.* 2:9–12).

This passage in 1 Peter re-echoes Exodus 19:4–6 and embodies the essential thrust of the third commandment. Those brought out of darkness into the wonderful light of the true

God, and who have received his mercy, must show the reality of that change by living before him without deceit and hypocrisy (*1 Pet.* 2:1).

ALLAN HARMAN

THE BOTTOM LINE

• God deserves to be honoured in our actions as well as our words.

• We should consider it a great privilege and honour to know and respect the only God of the universe.

• We need to keep a close eye on how we live as Christians because inconsistency and hypocrisy are violations of the third commandment.

7

THE FOURTH COMMANDMENT

Remember the Sabbath day, to keep it holy. Six days you shall labour, and do all your work, but the seventh day is a Sabbath to the LORD your God. On it you shall not do any work, you, or your son, or your daughter, your male servant, or your female servant, or your livestock, or the sojourner who is within your gates. For in six days the LORD made heaven and earth, the sea, and all that is in them, and rested the seventh day. Therefore the LORD blessed the Sabbath day and made it holy (Exod. 20:8–11).

Ever since the resurrection of Christ, the first day of the week has had great significance for Christians. However, the average believer of our generation has far less appreciation for this special day than those of past centuries. To understand the Bible's teaching on the pattern and use of the first day of the week we need to return to the beginning of time.

CREATION REST

The creation of time is not specifically mentioned in Genesis 1. However, no other aspect of God's universe is referred to as much in that passage as time. God's measurement of the passing of days is carefully recorded (1:5, 8, 13, etc.), and the sun and the moon are provided for us to carry on these calculations (1:14–19). At the beginning of Genesis 2 we observe the amazing spectacle of the God who could so effortlessly create everything resting to provide an example and to establish a pattern for those made in his image to follow (2:1–3). This hallowed or 'special' time is always to be distinguished from 'general' time and is called the 'Sabbath'. As a part of the very order of the creation, the moral principle of the Sabbath is understood to be a 'creation ordinance'.

The fourth commandment, as recorded in Exodus 20:8–11, requires us to recall the example of our Creator: 'For in six days the Lord made heaven and earth, the sea, and all that is in them, and rested the seventh day. Therefore the Lord blessed the Sabbath day and made it holy.'

'Sabbath' means 'rest, cessation from labour'. Although linked with the 'seventh' day in the fourth commandment, the word itself is not related or tied to the number seven. This is why, in the outworking of the plan of redemption, there can be a shift in the application of the command from the seventh to the first day of the week.

The idea of the 'seventh day' was tied to God's example. Upon the completion of his work in the first creation, God rested. We follow this seventh-day resting as a part of God's order right into the tomb of the Lord Jesus. The only complete twenty-four hour period that Christ's body was buried was the seventh day of the week (*Mark* 15:42–16:2). Jesus, as the Lord of the Sabbath (*Matt.* 12:8), provides a modified example for us to follow. The Sabbath principle is applied to the day of Christ's resurrection, the first day of the redeemed and new creation and the first step towards the never-ending rest, joy, and satisfaction of eternity.

REDEMPTION REST

The connection of the Sabbath with God's work of redemption is found as early as the reiteration of the Ten Commandments in Deuteronomy 5. The Sabbath command is unique in that the two instances where it is found give entirely different reasons for its observance. In Deuteronomy 5:12–15, the original creation is replaced by redemption: 'You shall remember that you were a slave in the land of Egypt, and the LORD your God brought you out from there with a mighty hand and an outstretched arm. Therefore the LORD your God commanded you to keep the Sabbath day.'

The identification of the Sabbath with redemption is completed with Jesus' resurrection. The principle of resting and enjoying God's gift of creation continues, but the old creation has been superseded by the new creation. The new creation is formed in the reverse order. It begins, on the first day of the week, with the victorious rest provided in Christ's finished work, continues with the creation of a new people, and will culminate at the end of history in the final renewal of the heavens and the earth.

As the author of the new creation Jesus ministers the benefits of his saving work through the Word and the Sacraments. This is seen in the repeated revelation of Jesus on the first day of the week, both before his ascension (*Matt.* 28:1–8; *Mark* 16:1–8; *Luke* 24:1–49; *John* 20:1–29) and afterwards (*Acts* 2; *Rev.* 1:10). This is why the early church continued to meet on the first day (*Acts* 20:7; *1 Cor.* 16:2).

In the same way that Jesus visited his disciples on the first day, we are to expect a special visitation from Jesus as we gather with his people to meet with him. This occasion is called *the Lord's Day* (*Rev.* 1:10) and the doctrine is known as the 'Christian Sabbath' (*Westminster Confession of Faith*, XXI: 7–8).

The claim is often made that the practice of Christians meeting on the first day is based on custom and not on command. This can easily be answered by the fact that whether we look to the first chapter of Genesis or to the Gospels and Acts, the strength of the Sabbath commandment is the divine character and example. The commandment, as it is found in Exodus and Deuteronomy, is dependent on God's character and example and not the other way around. Therefore, post-resurrection believers have as much warrant and obligation for observing the Sabbath on the first day according to the Redeemer's example as pre-resurrection believers did on the seventh day according to the Creator's example. Perhaps this is seen most clearly in the early church's practice of holding its 'holy convocations' or 'sacred assemblies' (*Lev.* 23:3) on the first day of the week. This often-overlooked reference lies behind the transfer of distinctly 'Sabbatarian' activities from the seventh day to the first day on the basis of Jesus' example and ministry.

MEETING WITH JESUS

We must, however, recognize that, in addition to the transition from the seventh day to the first day, the day itself has been radically changed and glorified. Any ceremonial shadow of the old order has been replaced with the fulfilment and the reality of Jesus. We no longer meet at an altar to offer sacrifices that prefigure Christ. We meet with the Lord himself! We rejoice in his final and effectual offering for sin. The original meaning of the expression 'Divine Service' is not that we serve God in worship, but that God serves us.

He ministers to us. He provides salvation and grace for our every need. We, in turn, go forth to serve him in the remaining days of the week.

Another ceremonial dimension of the Old Testament Sabbath that has ceased is that we no longer wait for our eternal rest to be secured. In Jesus we have already entered into it. However, we have not yet entered into the final realization of it in the age to come. This is why the writer to the Hebrews says, 'So then, there remains a Sabbath rest for the people of God' (*Heb.* 4:9). The word used here for 'rest' is unique in the New Testament. Consistent with the Septuagint (the ancient Greek translation of the Old Testament), it ought to be translated 'sabbath-keeping'. 'So then, there remains a sabbath-keeping for the people of God.' We must persevere in our Christian profession, which includes Sabbath-keeping as a fruit of our new life and our rest in Christ, if we are to enjoy that final and eternal rest that Jesus has secured.

MORE TO CELEBRATE

The significance of the Sabbath is not diminished in the new creation order but increased. We have more to celebrate, more to enjoy, and more reason to lay our other labours and activities aside than those who lived in the shadows of the old order. The promise of Isaiah 58:13–14 has even greater prospect for us than it did for its first hearers:

> If you turn back your foot from the Sabbath,
> from doing your pleasure on my holy day,
> and call the Sabbath a delight
> and the holy day of the LORD honourable;
> if you honour it, not going your own ways,
> or seeking your own pleasure, or talking idly;

then you shall take delight in the LORD,
and I will make you ride on the heights of the earth;
I will feed you with the heritage of Jacob your father,
for the mouth of the LORD has spoken.

The common attitude of seeing the Lord's Day as a depriv-ation of enjoyment or a denial of liberty could not be more misplaced. The Sabbath is not a subtraction; it is a glorious addition to our lives. It is a gracious gift of our merciful God. It is a day of rest from our labours and 'general' activities for the 'special' activities of worship, celebration, and fellowship.

How this is applied in detail will vary from church to church, family to family, and believer to believer, yet there are some broad concepts that we will share, and in this sense a 'Sabbath culture' is very useful. However, specific details will vary, and we must never legalistically put our own 'house rules' on the same level as 'God's rules'. We ought to respect and encourage one another as we all seek to make the most of, and live out the spirit of, the fourth commandment.

FINDING REST IN A RESTLESS WORLD

The Lord's Day is, sadly, one of the most neglected evangel-istic tools of our time. So often when the world wonders what the church has to offer and the church struggles to 'be noticed' in the right sense, confusion regarding the fourth commandment leads to missed opportunities. A positive and distinct observance of the Lord's Day will show others that we have found rest in a restless world.

There are 'general' activities that remain essential even on the Lord's Day. Rather than contradict the Sabbath, these serve and promote Sabbath observance. These include medical and security services, and are summarized in the

Westminster Confession as 'works of necessity and mercy'. Again, we follow the divine example of Jesus when he saved life on the Sabbath (*Mark* 3:1–5).

Our natural sinful tendency is always to make excuses and see other things as 'necessary' when they are not. God is sovereign over our time, work, and rest. Although the fourth commandment does state that we ought to be diligent in our work six days of the week, the focus of the command is rest. When we say, 'I must, I have to work', God replies, 'You must, you have to rest.' Our own work can never save us, nor can we ever make progress by compromising or rationalizing God's commands. In the same way, if our focus is on pursuing 'general' entertainment and 'recreations' on the Lord's Day, we are implying that our Saviour's ordained 'special' Sabbath activities are insufficient to 're-create' us and that we have insufficient faith, interest, and pleasure in them.

As a creation ordinance and a moral law, the Sabbath commandment is woven into the very fabric of life. Our physical, mental, emotional and, most importantly, spiritual health require the Sabbath. The divine example of Genesis 1 also reveals the need to structure our time and responsibilities so that they become our servants, not our masters. We are to have a plan and purpose for our days, while always submitting to the intervention of God's plan and purpose when his differs from ours (*James* 4:13–16). Perhaps more than any other commandment, we need to recover the treasure of the Bible's teaching on the Christian Sabbath. It is the weekly feast day of our Saviour who calls us to celebrate with him. Let us, as individuals, families and churches embrace and enjoy the Lord's Day as the blessing God intended it to be.

ANDREW CLARKE

THE BOTTOM LINE

• Because of the core principles of the fourth commandment, the inferential evidence in the New Testament, and the theological implications of the resurrection and future eternal rest, the application of this commandment has been transferred to Sunday, the Lord's Day.

• This commandment provides us with extra time and space to spend refreshing and revitalizing our connections to God the Creator and Jesus the Saviour, our reason for living and our hope for the future.

• Because the Sabbath (the Lord's Day) was made for man, it should be a day of delight (*Isa.* 58:13–14), not a day of burdensome boredom.

• Practically speaking, the Lord's Day is:

a day for focusing on and delighting in the one and only living God;

a day for resting from the regular chores of the week, but not a day of laziness;

a day for relationships, fellowship, and doing good to other people.

8

THE FIFTH COMMANDMENT

Honour your father and your mother, that your days may be long in the land that the LORD your God is giving you (Exod. 20:12).

FAMILY TROUBLES

Cultures both West and East need to hear the fifth commandment afresh. In western societies 'children's rights' has become a banner under which the legitimate role of parenting is undermined. Since the 1960s many western countries have seen an open questioning of authority of all kinds, including a rejection of parental authority and a redefinition of the structure of the family.

In the Asian context there is the tendency for parents to seek to control their children, even into adulthood. Giving renewed attention to the teaching of the fifth commandment will help lead us out of the moral morass we have brought upon ourselves.

DIVINE STRUCTURE

The Ten Commandments are not given in just any order, rather there is a logic to the way they are listed, with the first four dealing with our relationship with God and the last six with our relationship with our fellow-man. These two aspects, which we might call religious duty and moral duty respectively, are vitally related. The fourth commandment helps to build a bridge between the first four and the last six commandments.

The observance of the Sabbath is clearly part of our service for God and so belongs with the first three commandments ('The seventh day is a sabbath to the LORD your God'), but it also instructs us on part of our responsibility to son, daughter, servants, and others, who are to be allowed to share our rest from work.

The fifth commandment also helps to bind the first four and the last six commandments together. It is the commandment that is most similar to the first four, because it presents parents as authority figures, and to that extent 'God-like'.

PARENTS 'PLAYING GOD'

Now parents are not God. They are not to 'play God', and we are not to make our parents 'God'; but still they have a role in teaching us right from wrong and passing on to us the instructions of God. This is a responsibility that is greatly stressed in Deuteronomy (4:9–10; 6:4–9) and by Paul (*Eph.* 6:4). Parents need to recognize the increasing moral responsibility and independence of their children as they grow and mature.

Ephesians 6:4 indicates that this commandment is as much for parents as for children. While parents are in a 'God-like role', especially when children are young, they are to lead in God-like ways and avoid all tendencies towards despotic authoritarianism. Jesus clearly showed us a way of leadership that was contrary to the ways of the world (*John* 13:12–15; *1 Pet.* 5:1–4). Those who exasperate their children by their despotic, careless or cruel parenting will be held accountable by God. Parents need to heed the warning of Jesus not to cause little ones to stumble (*Luke* 17:1–3).

On the other hand, the parent is 'like God', and a proper attitude to our parents bears a striking resemblance to our attitude to God. We must 'honour' our parents, that is, respect and revere them, which are attitudes (and actions) we associate with a proper relation to God.

A few Bible references will establish this fact. 'Every one of you shall revere his mother and his father, and you shall keep my Sabbaths' (*Lev.* 19:3). 'You shall stand up before the grey head and honour the face of an old man, and you shall fear your God' (*Lev.* 19:32). Both these passages juxtapose duty to parents and duty to God. 'A son honours his father, and a servant his master. If then I am a father, where is my honour? And if I am a master, where is my fear?' (*Mal.* 1:6).

If God calls himself a father, then parents must be 'like God' (the analogy works in both directions). Parents are to be honoured in a 'God-like' way. We have no excuse not to honour our parents, and that means above all to be willing to learn from them. 'Listen to your father who gave you life, and do not despise your mother when she is old' (*Prov.* 23:22).

The most important priority after a right relationship with God is a right relationship with parents. This is an obvious implication of the positioning of the fifth commandment immediately after the first four. Every parent has something of value to pass on to his or her children, and though many parents do not follow their own precepts, we are to be open to what our parents can teach us.

A QUESTION OF PRIORITIES

This is the first human relationship specifically focused on in the Ten Commandments because it is fundamental to all relationships. We did not have to wait for modern schools of psychology to learn that early childhood experiences and choices affect a person throughout life. Freud saw the supreme importance of the parent-child relationship but of course misunderstood its significance because he did not consult Scripture on the subject.

Psychological problems result if parents are overly restrictive and repressive, but problems also arise if a child is particularly rebellious or resents and rejects his or her parents' authority. If we do not honour our parents, we not only displease God, we bring harm upon ourselves.

Children should honour their parents by recognizing the burden of responsibility that has been placed upon them by God. Those who experience unfair, cruel, or abusive parenting can take some comfort in the fact that such parents will have to answer to God for their actions.

Nevertheless, God does not say only honour 'good' parents. If we want to be happy and healthy we must forgive our parents for sinning against us and be still willing to learn from them.

Psychologists are right when they say that if there is something wrong in our relationship with our parents, we will be adversely affected and all our relationships will be (at least to some extent) impaired. The problem is not only that our parents sinned against us, but that we have added our sin to theirs and have not forgiven them and honoured them. Forgiveness is the biblical remedy that modern psychology cannot supply!

ONLY FOR LITTLE CHILDREN?

Is this commandment only for little children? It is certainly applicable to the child (as *Eph.* 6:1–4 shows), but is this commandment different from the other nine which are for adults? Is this the one commandment out of the ten with a 'sunset clause', so that when a person reaches eighteen or twenty-one years of age it no longer applies? Jesus makes reference to this commandment in application to an adult (*Mark* 7:9–13), so that one implication of the commandment is a continuing responsibility to support our parents if they have physical or other needs: this is what it means to 'honour' them at an advanced stage of life.

This commandment is of relevance as long as we have parents, though the form of the application must and will change as years go by. The parent-child relationship goes through various phases, but a person is never too old to hold his or her parents in honour. Any person with living parents comes under this commandment, and the commandment especially has in mind how mature adults are to treat their older or elderly parents. Our parents most need our respect and support when they reach the later years of life (*1 Tim.* 5:3–8).

THE COMMANDMENT WITH A PROMISE

We are given a promise to encourage us in our efforts (a point noted by Paul in Ephesians 6:2). This goes with the fact that it is one of only two commandments within the ten that are expressed positively. Longevity is the reward for those who care for elderly parents ('that your days may be long in the land that the LORD your God is giving you'), this being a 'measure-for-measure' type of reward. Faithful sons and daughters who care for parents will themselves grow old and be taken care of. It is true of course! Our children learn how to treat us from the way we treat our parents! The child-grandparent relationship is an important one for a child. Our children will take notice if we dishonour their grandparents.

AUTHORITY IN SOCIETY

As with all the commandments, it is difficult to restrict the range of the application of the fifth commandment. Out of the authority of parents, all other authority is derived and develops, so that the attitude of children to their parents affects the health of society as a whole (*Rom.* 1:30).

Deuteronomy 16:18–18:22 provides an exposition of the fifth commandment and shows its wide-ranging application to the authority figures of ancient Israelite society: the judge, the king, the priest, and the prophet. In dealing with these four groups, the movement is backwards through the line of authority which starts with God communicating his instructions by the prophets. After this, priests have the responsibility of instructing the people concerning the word of God, and then kings have the responsibility of setting up and maintaining a system of justice. Finally, judges have the responsibility of enforcing the system that has been set up. Thus the way that Israel was governed was an outworking of this commandment.

POWER-SHARING

Just as authority was shared by the two parents, father and mother, not centred in only one individual, so this distribution of authority and power carries over into a decentralization and limitation of authority among judges, kings, priests and prophets. We could express the Deuteronomic ideal as that of 'power-sharing', with the severe delimitation most notable in the case of the king who is not allowed to act as a despot. The Bible does not mandate a particular form of government for the modern era, but principles such as justice for all, the sharing of power, and laws based on biblical morality have abiding applications. Thus home life, social life, work life and political life are all within the scope of the fifth commandment.

SWEEPING APPLICATION

The book of Deuteronomy does the same with each of the Ten Commandments in turn (*Deut.* 12–26), and its applications cover almost every conceivable area of life. The same kind of 'free-wheeling' interpretation of the commandments is given in the *Westminster Larger* and *Shorter Catechisms,* which apply the fifth commandment to all social relations, whether with 'superiors, inferiors, or equals' (*Shorter Catechism,* Question 63). The approach taken is the exact opposite to legalism, which seeks to restrict the moral implications of God's commandments to narrowly defined areas. The fifth commandment has implications for how husbands and wives treat each other (*Eph.* 5:21–33), for how parents and children relate together (*Eph.* 6:1–4), for the cooperation of master and slave (*Eph.* 6:5–9), for those who govern and are governed (*Rom.* 13:1–7), and for how people behave in the life of the church (*Rom.* 12:10). The whole of life can be viewed as the out-working of the fifth commandment.

GREG GOSWELL

THE BOTTOM LINE

• The fifth commandment is for the promotion of stable, healthy families which will naturally promote more contented and orderly societies.

• There are responsibilities for parents as well as children in this commandment and these principles are generally applicable to all relationships where there are leaders and followers.

• As we live in an imperfect world, parents and children need to understand the importance of forgiveness in the process of maintaining honour, respect, stability and orderliness within families.

9

THE SIXTH COMMANDMENT

You shall not murder (Exod. 20:13).

QUESTIONS AND DILEMMAS

What is wrong with suicide? Should scientists kill animals in experimentations? Should we support or oppose capital punishment? Can killing ever be justified? Does abortion involve murder? These are just some of the questions and dilemmas that surround the sixth commandment.

READING THE TEN COMMANDMENTS TODAY

The Christian approach to the Ten Commandments is:

• to discover what each commandment enshrines as its essential moral principle.

• to read it in the light of the whole of Scripture, especially God's personal revelation in Jesus Christ.

So what lies behind the Sixth Commandment? There is a rich, multi-levelled background to it.

God himself lies behind it. This is because the God of the Bible is the living God, the Author of all life since creation (*John* 1:1–3). As the living God he has life in himself and presents himself as the Living One. This must mean that God is always on the side of living things, their protection and support. The creation story of Genesis 1 amply illustrates this principle of God's delight in life. God appoints and brings into being living creatures in earth, and sea and sky, of every imaginable type: plants and trees, land animals, fish, birds, and lastly human beings.

So what about death? Death is an alien experience, the product of personal cosmic evil rising against the God of the universe and drawing humankind into the same rebellion. As a result we live in a disordered, pain-filled world, for which human beings are only partly responsible (*Gen.* 2:15–3:19).

The special kind of life given to humanity lies behind it. God made man like no other creature. God chose his own image as the template for humanity (*Gen.* 1:26–28). As God's image-bearers, even after the Fall into sin (*James* 3:9), human beings are particularly precious. As we shall see below, it is only under carefully prescribed circumstances that human life may ever be terminated.

The secular ethicist Peter Singer has argued against the reasons underpinning special protection being extended to members of the human family (what he calls *speciesism,* and regards as a moral fault like racism or sexism). His larger aim has been to demolish the traditional Christian ethics of the West. His nearer aim has been to raise public consciousness of other species whose differences from man may only be relative.

The strongest defence against Singer's critique is the Christian belief in the divine image in humanity. For non-religious people in our society this belief carries little author-ity. Yet most people instinctively react against the wanton destruction of human life (as in war, for example) and so in practice adhere to a belief in the sanctity of human life.

The gracious gift of eternal life lies behind it. John 3:16 is the best known verse in the Bible and by itself sums up the purpose of God for the world. The choice is between life and death. God sent his Son to secure life for us. This life is available in Jesus Christ for those who put their trust in him. God made us for himself and our hearts are restless until they find their rest in God.

Perhaps the best support for belief in the uniqueness and worth of human lives is the event of the incarnation when God took human nature to himself and came into the world as the historical individual, Jesus of Nazareth. The conception and birth of Jesus, the God-Man, tells us more clearly than any other event that God values and cares for human life above all other life-forms (including angels) to be found throughout the universe.

ARE THERE EXCEPTIONS TO THE SIXTH COMMANDMENT?

The sixth commandment speaks out against the sin of murder, not killing *per se*. Murder is a deliberate elimination of another image-bearer, for reasons of passion, hate, jealousy or fanaticism, and usually with premeditation. The Bible differentiates murder from acts of manslaughter in which people are accidentally killed (*Num.* 35:9–34). Manslaughter and murder bring about the same result in the loss of human life, but the motives leading to these acts are not the same.

Christian ethical teaching has usually qualified the terms of the sixth commandment in three instances. In each of these three cases, killing finds justification within a larger framework of accountability and the greater good.

The legitimate killing of those who side with evil powers in war (Deut. 20:1–18). This is the ethical tradition of the just war that Augustine first defended. One may think here of evil regimes like those of Hitler, Stalin, Milosevic, and Mugabe. Politicians, soldiers and civilians who support such regimes share in their evil and deserve to suffer with them.

Self-defence that unintentionally leads to the death of an attacker has traditionally been permitted in cases of housebreaking and robbery. Regrettably, the law as it stands in several western countries is on the side of the attacker not the victim and house-owner, who may be held liable for any injury to the intruder.

Capital punishment is more controversial. Secularists oppose it on the ground that it is inhumane, or religious people (for example, Roman Catholics) may oppose it because thay believe that it is unworthy of God's universal love. But the Bible holds that there are capital offences (e.g. *Lev.* 20:10, 13–14; *Deut.* 22:24).

When God reorganized the earth after the Flood he appointed this ordinance because sin threatened human survival (*Gen.* 9:6). The murderer strikes at God himself through destroying one of his image-bearers.

The death of Christ is the supreme example of the death penalty. We deserved to die but he took our place and died instead (*1 Pet.* 3:18; see also *Luke* 23:40–41). Paul was willing to die for any crime deserving death (*Acts* 25:1).

WHAT DOES THE SIXTH COMMANDMENT MEAN IN PRACTICE?

All God's commands have a negative and positive side to them. The sixth commandment is no exception. Negatively, the sixth commandment challenges all thoughts and words that are of murderous intention, such as outbursts of anger, jealousy, self-love, unjust discrimination, being partisan, an unforgiving spirit and aggression (*Matt.* 5:21–26). This commandment relates to everyday people in everyday life as it addresses the way we relate to and interact with people. By relating this commandment even to our thought life, Jesus shows us that none of us can escape the need to be constantly mindful of its deeper applications.

In a special way the sixth commandment is relevant to the practice of medicine today and is opposed to its culture of death.

It applies:

Before human life begins. Married couples ought not to restrict unduly or prevent altogether their reproductive powers. Sex is for pleasure but also for reproductive purposes (*Gen.* 1:26–28; 2:18–25).

Once human life has begun. At conception human embryos ought to be allowed to continue their individual human journeys uninterrupted. Embryos are the most vulnerable of our neighbours whom we ought to love unconditionally.

When life is under way. No foetus should be sacrificed for the sake of another human being, except in the quite exceptional case of the mother's life being at risk. Most abortions take place for social and personal convenience or as a belated contraceptive.

When human life is full-grown. People should live life as a gift that neither they nor anyone else should terminate. No-one has the right to die. Suicide is never justified morally, however meaningless, depressing, lonely or painful life has become. Life is a human good that no set of circumstances can render worthless.

When human life reaches its end. People ought not to terminate their own lives by euthanasia, nor should governments legalize such a procedure. The same ethical reasons stand against euthanasia as stand against suicide. Even in the face of the tragic loss of human dignity, God alone has the right to bring the life of an individual to a close (*Job* 1:20–21). As death approaches we are taught by the example of Jesus to entrust our lives into the Lord's hands (*Luke* 23:46).

In addition to the above, Christians should lament the sacrifice of human life in the service of supposed cures for life-threatening illnesses. IVF and embryonic stem cell research illustrate the growing acceptance of this sacrifice of human life.

Positively, the sixth commandment means being pro-actively pro-life in a host of ways and contexts, summed up in the popular saying, 'Life. Be in it!' In an increasingly adversarial and violent world Christians need to be salt and light in procreating, preserving, and defending human life and living things. This goal can be achieved in practical terms by, for example, giving blood, becoming a life-guard, a police officer, a doctor or a surgeon, caring for the dying, sharing the gospel, loving and serving others, caring for animals, protecting the environment, or generally being like Jesus, who 'went about doing good' (*Acts* 10:38). It also means that in moral dilemmas, like that of Rahab (*Josh.* 2:1–7), we put saving human lives above every other moral precept. The 'right to life' is a secular dogma which borrows its moral capital from a Christian heritage that secularists aim to overthrow. Still, human life is a universal good that should never normally be set aside. Even a criminal deserves a fair trial, and a prisoner of war deserves humane treatment.

DOUGLAS MILNE

THE BOTTOM LINE

• This commandment is about the value and sanctity of human life and is therefore relevant even for the most complex ethical dilemmas of our time.

• When applied positively this means that we should seek to protect and preserve human life, treating it with dignity at all times.

• Jesus' application of this commandment brought it into everyday life by showing that it also applies to how we think and talk about people.

IO

THE SEVENTH COMMANDMENT

You shall not commit adultery (Exod. 20:14).

KEEPING OUR COMMITMENTS

The seventh commandment speaks to the very heart of our personhood and our relationships. To break the seventh commandment is to commit an act of betrayal in the most intimate human relationship we can have. It affects deeply a very minimum of three people, usually many more involving whole families and communities.

THE MEANING OF THE SEVENTH COMMANDMENT

The commandment itself: 'You shall not commit adultery', consists of only two little words in Hebrew, as it is stated in Exodus 20:14 and Deuteronomy 5:18. One of those words is the negative. The other word is the second person singular imperative of the verb that refers specifically to the act of a married person breaking the vows of his or her marriage covenant by becoming involved intimately with another (usually also married) person. Primarily, sexual intercourse would be in mind, although, by far the greatest usage of the word in the Old Testament is in the context of idolatry, or spiritual unfaithfulness to the LORD and his covenant with Israel. The word therefore has a much wider application than just the physical act of intercourse, and covers the whole emotional aspect of human relationships (see *Matt.* 2:28; 15:19; *Mark* 7:21).

This emphasis should not surprise us. Marriage, as 'a holy estate, instituted by God', is clearly intended to have a wider purpose than simply providing a framework in which men and women can express their feelings for each other and in which children can be created and nurtured. It is intended to 'signify the mystical union between Christ and his church'. The seventh commandment, therefore, has far wider implications than just what the physical aspect might suggest. It is addressing our whole attitude to commitments and relationships, warning us against the abuse of one another's persons, emotions, trust, and so on, for the sake of gratifying our own desires and lusts, in the spiritual as well as the physical realm.

THE CHALLENGE OF THE 21ST CENTURY

The seventh commandment ought to be of special interest and concern to us today. For the most part, our society does not treat it as having relevance any more to the way we live. Even television shows and movies considered 'family-friendly' include themes and incidents that totally ignore the clear teaching of God's Word about faithfulness and the sanctity of marriage.

We used to debate whether two people firmly committed to each other should engage in sex before they were married; now we treat co-habitation, with or without the intention of marriage, as the normally accepted arrangement. Extramarital affairs are considered part of the complex nature of living and relationships, and are even prescribed as therapy by some marriage counsellors.

HOW SHOULD WE AS CHRISTIANS RESPOND TO THIS MASSIVE SHIFT IN ATTITUDES?

A young man, talking about the Bible's teaching and the shift in thinking even among Christians, commented to me: 'You can't tell me your generation didn't do some of these things when you were young – human nature has always been the same!' My response was that this is so, but the very significant difference is that when we were doing it we knew we were doing the wrong thing!

God not only gives us this commandment in his Word, he also gives us many practical situations that demonstrate its importance. David was Israel's greatest ever king. The Lord chose him as king because he was 'a man after his own heart' (*1 Sam.* 13:14). But David's breaking of the seventh commandment with Bathsheba brought God's judgment upon him. Apart from the fact that David had already broken the tenth commandment by coveting his neighbour's wife, his sin also led to his breaking at least two other commandments in order to 'cover up' its consequences: he deceived Bathsheba's husband by trying to set up a situation where it would look like the conceived baby was Uriah's (the ninth commandment), and then 'arranged' for Uriah's death in battle (the sixth commandment) so that he would be free to marry Bathsheba.

David's actions were a clear demonstration of James' inference, that breaking one commandment is equivalent to breaking them all (*James* 2:10–11). This incident (*2 Sam.* 11) and Nathan's exposing of it (*2 Sam.* 12) are enough to prove the timeless relevance of the seventh commandment. It is not without significance that Paul instructed Timothy and Titus that one of the requirements of an elder or deacon is that he be *the husband of but one wife* (*1 Tim.* 3:2, 12; *Titus* 1:6). Any sexual activity outside its designed confinement to a married couple (one man and one woman) is clearly never reported or discussed in Scripture with approval. The seventh commandment encapsulates this truth.

We live in a society that treats sex completely differently from this. It appears that the generally approved view is that sex is merely a physical activity, to be enjoyed whenever consenting people feel it is appropriate, without a concern for long-term commitment, and with ways of controlling the consequences. 'Casual sex' is an accepted recreational past-time. On this basis, relationships involving sex are not treated necessarily as permanent or exclusive. People quite happily live together in a 'trial marriage', as if it were a wise thing to see whether it works before sealing it as permanent. We talk about 'partners' instead of husbands and wives. A generation ago the question of sex before marriage, between a man and a woman who had made a vow to love each other exclusively 'till death us do part', was a live issue in our society. Sadly, changing attitudes to marriage have made this less the case today, so that now even opinion among professing Christians is divided.

While it might be argued that true commitment is a private matter of the heart, and therefore a couple can consider themselves 'married' in God's eyes without a formal ceremony, and, conversely, that a ceremony in itself does not make an authentic marriage, it would seem clear that God's commandments, and his principles for marriage, are meant to be public concerns.

Therefore, in the light of Paul's injunction, 'abstain from all appearance of evil' (*1 Thess.* 5:22, KJV), it ought to be acknowledged that sexual activity without a publicly recognized marriage is not within the bounds of what God approves.

REDEMPTIVE HISTORY AND THE SEVENTH COMMANDMENT

Probably the place where the seventh commandment has its most important application in redemptive history concerns the relationship between Christ and his church. The introduction to the Marriage Service says: 'Marriage is a holy estate, instituted by God. The Scriptures hold it in the highest regard, commending it to all people, and consecrating it because it signifies the mystical union between Christ and his church.' God's institution of marriage is clearly intended to help us understand our spiritual relationship with him. It is more than just symbolic that the prophets called the worship of other gods 'adultery'. Christians, therefore, have a very important responsibility with regard to marriage. God makes it clear in the Scriptures that sexual intimacy is intended and permitted only within the confines of an established and recognized marriage relationship. The seventh commandment protects this provision.

Jesus' command in Matthew 5 takes it a step further and warns that the actual problem begins in the mind even before it shows itself physically. Followers of Jesus must deal with the sin of adultery at this point. So at the level of human relationships, marriage is meant for our good – our protection and happiness. But Christian marriage also portrays to a watching world a picture of Christ's relationship to his church.

We therefore have a greater responsibility to ensure that our marriages are healthy and openly so. The pattern of the first three commandments is to be reflected in marriage. No other gods means no other wives, official or unofficial; no images means no lustful looks at or thoughts towards other women – not even, or especially not, quick glimpses on the internet or through 'harmless' interludes or verbal dalliances in chat rooms; not misusing the name of the Lord means honesty, faithfulness, devotion, and honour towards my wife's person and reputation. In the light of this, even the fourth commandment perhaps suggests that we should set aside a regular time to express our exclusive devotion to our spouses in order to ensure an open, healthy relationship!

BRUCE CHRISTIAN

THE BOTTOM LINE

- The positive heart of this commandment is to define the proper context for sex and to promote God's design for marriage.

- Focusing on the positive heart of this commandment allows us to evaluate a wide range of relationship issues and all matters of sexuality: faithfulness in marriage, divorce, re-marriage, polygamy, incest, homosexuality, co-habitation, *de facto* relationships, wife-swapping, how to treat a wife, how to treat a husband, modest dress codes, and so on.

- We should be glad that God has given us this commandment, as it protects us from harm and promotes the happy, healthy relationships we all need and crave. When we violate the principles of this commandment it is like putting hot coals in our laps (*Prov.* 6:27), taking something good and misusing it in a way that hurts us. Life's painful experiences tell us that God is right.

II

THE EIGHTH COMMANDMENT

You shall not steal (Exod. 20:15).

AGAINST THE CULTURE

We live in a 'must have' culture. We are constantly bombarded by messages from advertisers telling us that we 'need the latest . . .', 'life would be so much easier with . . .', 'if you don't have . . . then you are out of step', or 'you should buy . . . because you deserve it'. Added to this is the pressure to climb the social ladder (often measured by possessions) and in the process we are tempted to constantly measure our progress against our neighbours.

Modern society plays upon our natural covetousness, creating a level of dissatisfaction that leaves us always wanting more. This is what keeps the economy spinning, and if we buy more than we need, it spins all the faster. But the breeding of covetousness also leads to people satisfying their wants by illegal means.

Whilst as Christians we would acknowledge the need to keep the eighth commandment, we still may be tempted to think we are owed something. We may never consider robbing a bank, but who has not been faced with the moral dilemma of being mistakenly under-charged for goods or receiving too much change from a shopkeeper: has the Lord marvellously provided? Despite our tendency to rationalize, the Lord does not provide in ways that contravene his own Word, and his standard is uncompromising: 'You shall not steal.'

JUST TWO SMALL WORDS?

In the Hebrew language, in which Moses received the eighth commandment, it is written with just two small words, yet they are packed with meaning and have potentially far-reaching application, especially since the commandment has no object (we are not told what we shall not steal). This has led to much discussion over what God intended and a confusing overlap with other commandments.

Yet, it seems clear from the examples within the law itself that material possessions (whether goods *or people*, given that slavery was an unpleasant fact of life) are particularly in mind.

As we reflect upon the commandment, we find both positive and negative implications.

Positively, it affirms a person's right to private property, and places an onus upon us to respect the property of others and their right to enjoy it. So the land of Canaan was divided among the tribes, clans, and families of Israel, each receiving their own portion.

Beyond this, the commandment affirms the virtue of earning a living by honest work, and the responsibility to use all that we have wisely, not just for our own benefit, but also for the well-being of those in need. When the Israelites were given the land of Canaan it was so that they might work the land and enjoy its produce; yet while so doing, they were to remember that everything they had was on trust from the Lord. It therefore came with a responsibility to be generous in providing for the needs of those who were aliens, fatherless, or widows (*Deut.* 24:19–22).

Turning to the New Testament, we find that Paul also affirms the value of honest work. He denounces the Cretans for being 'lazy gluttons' (*Titus* 1:12) and espouses the biblical principle that 'If anyone is not willing to work, let him not eat' (*2 Thess.* 3:10). We also witness the generosity of Christians who provided for those in need, sometimes even before the need arose (*Acts* 4:32–37; 11:27–30).

Negatively, the commandment forbids stealing another person's possessions. It literally forbids anyone 'to carry away' (by stealth) something that belongs to another without that person's consent.

Within the law of Moses there are specific examples that help explain the principle contained in the eighth commandment. A person is not to steal livestock (*Exod.* 22:1–4), nor to steal pasture by grazing his livestock on someone else's land (*Exod.* 22:5). Stealing possessions (items of silver or gold) from a neighbour's house is forbidden (*Exod.* 22:7). If a person finds something that belongs to a neighbour (for example, an ox, donkey, or cloak) it is to be returned to him (*Exod.* 23:4; *Deut.* 22:1–3). The implication is that to keep it (or even to ignore it) is to steal from that neighbour.

The stealing of a person (kidnapping) is also forbidden and is punishable by death (*Deut.* 24:7).

The commandment also extends to business practices. In commerce, the Israelites were not to oppress or take advantage of a hired man when it comes to his wages (*Deut.* 24:14), nor to use dishonest weights to cheat customers (*Deut.* 25:13–16).

Where someone had stolen from another, a principle of restitution was to operate. The person who 'stole' was required to pay back (at least) double what he had taken (see, for example, *Exod.* 22:7). So in God's perfect justice, he lost an amount equal to that which he had hoped to gain.

In the context of the New Testament, the Ten Commandments are reaffirmed. The apostle Paul lists thieves among those who will not inherit the kingdom of God (*1 Cor.* 6:10). He denounces theft and affirms the positive alternative. In Romans 13:9–10 Paul reveals that another way of saying, 'You shall not steal', is, 'You shall love your neighbour as yourself', for, 'Love does no wrong to a neighbour.'

Paul brings together the negative prohibition and the positive affirmation of the command in Ephesians 4:28: 'Let the thief no longer steal, but rather let him labour, doing honest work with his own hands, so that he may have something to share with anyone in need.'

CONSEQUENCES OF NEGLECT

Jesus revealed (*Luke* 6:31) the standard requirement of God's love: 'As you wish that others would do to you, do so to them.' To ignore this leads to a fractured society. No society can operate harmoniously where there is not mutual respect for property. More fundamentally, however, neglect of the commandment results in broken relationships between people and God.

We see this clearly in the case of Judas Iscariot. He worshipped, prayed and preached, along with the other disciples, but John reveals that all along he was a thief, embezzling their collective funds (*John* 12:6). His greed eventually led him to betray his Lord for thirty pieces of silver. Despite the outward pretence, which could not fool Jesus, Judas had no fellowship with God and died forsaken by him. It is no surprise to find a widespread rejection of the Lord and his standards in societies that foster the kind of values that Judas embraced.

In our own society there is a strong belief in personal property, but at the same time little is done to encourage respect for the property of others. Those who heed God's voice are called to a different way. Their honesty is to be a breath of fresh air that brings blessing into the lives of others.

THE ALTERNATIVE: LIVING OUT THE COMMANDMENT

As with the other nine commandments, there is a general application to all people everywhere and in all times; most societies and cultures have laws against stealing. Yet, there is also a specific covenant sense in which the commandment speaks to Christians.

At the heart of this commandment is the requirement to trust in our covenant Lord for all our needs, recognizing that the God who feeds the birds of the air and clothes the lilies of the field will also see that our needs (not our wish-lists) are met, for we are so much more precious to him than birds and flowers. So, 'a generous God forbids his people to steal' (Raymond Brown). Embracing this truth leads to contentment and thankfulness (*Phil.* 4:11), whatever the size of our bank balance may be. At the same time, we recognize our responsibility to be productive members of society and, like our bountiful God, we are to be generous to others (with a particular responsibility to our fellow-believers).

Heeding the commandment will also keep us from wrong kinds of behaviour. For example, it will keep us from:

- idleness and laziness;
- keeping too much change when we realize the mistake;
- travelling on a train or tram without paying the fare;
- cheating in business and in our tax returns;
- grazing our livestock on someone else's land (yes, this can still be an issue today in rural areas);
- shifting boundary markers: Many have lost part of their land because a fence was (inadvertently or otherwise) built in the wrong place. In a particular case the landowner knew of the mistake, but kept quiet to his own advantage.
- ignoring, keeping, or failing to return something found which rightfully belongs to someone else;
- borrowing what we know we will not be able to pay back, for instance, the irresponsible use of credit cards;
- being uncharitable with our goods and wealth.

As God's covenant people, we are called to live in his way. How different our lives will be when, in the words of Thomas Boston, 'we deal with God as if the eyes of men were on us; and with men as knowing the eyes of God are on us'!

BARRY OAKES

THE BOTTOM LINE

- The positive side of this commandment protects the right of ownership.
- The application of this commandment relates to matters such as healthy personal boundaries, sharing, lending, respectful rules for borrowing, diligence in the work place and how we use talents and possessions for the kingdom of God.

• We should be thankful that God is concerned about justice in relation to what belongs to us, and we should remember to trust him to provide what we need.

12

THE NINTH COMMANDMENT

*You shall not bear false witness against
your neighbour* (Exod. 20:16).

RELATIVISM AND LIES

Ours is an age of intellectual relativism: the only truth is that which is true for me. Ours is an age of media hype: images and feelings are more important than a person's reputation. Ours is an age of unrestrained personal ambition, self-esteem, and selfishness: I deserve comfort and happiness, and will do whatever it takes to get it. The ninth commandment, therefore, directly collides with our post-modern culture, because this is the command about truth.

ORDER IN COURT!

'I swear to tell the truth, the whole truth, and nothing but the truth, so help me God.' This oath from the legal world summarizes the primary meaning of the ninth commandment. Israel at Mount Sinai was a newly formed theocracy, having just been redeemed from Egypt. She already had a rudimentary legal system, which involved the elders of the tribes and which lately had been centralized under Moses (*Exod.* 18).

With this background, the Lord formalizes and regulates one particular aspect of the nation's legal system, namely the role of the witness. The NIV brings out the legal force of the statement: 'You shall not give false testimony against your neighbour' (*Deut.* 19:15–21, where the idea of 'false witness' arises in a clearly legal context). When you stand in the witness box, you must not lie. Instead, positively, you must tell the truth. Despite the example of a former President of the United States who has been convicted of perjury, we can deduce that we are not to lie to the court even to save our own skin.

Why is the focus upon the witness and not the judge? At the heart of any legal system is the discovery of evidence, and evidence requires witnesses. Justice requires truth (*Lev.* 19:15–18; *Deut.* 24:16–25:16). More broadly, the command supports the concept of an orderly legal system for society. There must be a process to search out the facts. The witnesses must play their role, and the judge also. There must be a public hearing, oaths made, and a system of appeals, all of which are attested in the Pentateuch. The cause of justice is not served by a haphazard approach.

How important this commandment is for our modern (post-modern) society. There have been not-too-subtle attacks upon our system of law. The role of the jury has been questioned, for why should the opinion of twelve ignorant people have any validity in my life? Television shows like *Ally McBeal* have not helped, depicting the system as hopelessly quagmired in the narcissism of the protagonists (*2 Pet.* 2:10–11!). Added to this are the all-too-real cases of inadequate sentencing, revealing an uneasiness with the very concept of justice, and the craze of the outlandish malpractice suit, which turns the legal system into a high-stakes lottery.

Nevertheless, we can say upon the basis of the Word of God that we believe in the legal system. It operates under the mandate of God. The witnesses are not called to the stand by the prosecution, the defence, or even the judge. They are called there by God himself (see *Deut.* 1:17; the judgment is also God's).

Sometimes the system makes mistakes. There can be abuse and manipulation. Innocent people can be convicted. It is a *human* system, and only ever approximates to the justice of God. The Lord is well aware of this: the ninth commandment is predicated on the perversity of the human spirit. Still, it is God's system. Whilst the fullness of his justice belongs to the future age, the Lord endorses the human effort to make his justice intrude into the present (*Acts* 25:9–11; *Rom.* 13:1–7; *1 Tim.* 2:1–2; *Titus* 3:1; *1 Pet.* 2:13–17).

WE MUST HANDLE THE TRUTH!

In a classic film moment, in *A Few Good Men*, Jack Nicholson exclaims, 'You can't handle the truth.' The ninth commandment says not only that you *can* handle the truth, but that you *must* handle it! Moreover, this extends beyond the law courts. God is truth, and he requires those who bear his image to conform to his nature; so you must 'handle the truth' in all circumstances. This is essential for the proper functioning of society and for God-honouring personal relationships.

The extraction of this underlying principle is perhaps envisaged in Deuteronomy 5:20. In preaching through the law, Moses replaced the word 'false' with 'nothingness', 'emptiness' (*Exod.* 20:16, see also *Deut.* 5:20). A 'false witness' is given in a court of law, but an 'empty testimony' is anything that is said against one's neighbour (*Prov.* 12:17–19). At the very least, this change in vocabulary shows that the 'whole truth' is not just an absence of lies. Jesus kept silent during his trial, but gave the whole truth when placed under oath (*Matt.* 26:62–64).

PERSONAL IMPLICATIONS

What are the personal implications of the 'You shall not lie' principle? As the third commandment requires that we have a truthful relationship with the Lord, so too must we be truthful in all our dealings with our neighbour, with our enemies as with our friends, with those in authority over us, with our family, and so on.

We must tell the truth to our neighbour, and about our neighbour. We must not speak or act in a way that intends to deceive our neighbour.

A person listed 'gardening' as a hobby on his résumé. His sole efforts in this regard consisted of mowing the lawn once every two months. However, there is to be no 'gilding the lily', half-truths, little white lies, self-aggrandisement, media spin, sweet-talking the boss, buttering-up, soft-soaping, currying favour and so on.

Despite the ruling of the ancient Jewish tradition that it is permissible to lie to a tax collector, the ninth commandment prohibits cheating on your tax return. Proverbs 11:1 says, 'A false balance is an abomination to the LORD.' Racism and sexism are also forbidden, for these assert that others are less than they really are.

Neither are we to lie to ourselves. Contrary to some self-esteem psychology, a person is 'not to think of himself more highly than he ought to think' (*Rom.* 12:3). 'For if anyone thinks he is something, when he is nothing, he deceives himself' (*Gal.* 6:3).

IS IT ALWAYS WRONG TO LIE?

Is it ever right to tell a lie? The Nazi soldiers in your kitchen demand to know where you have hidden the Jewish family. What do you tell them? Despite the teaching of some of the most eminent church fathers, of course you lie! There are situations where some people cease to have a right to the truth, where a confidence has to be kept, or where a person almost ceases to be one's neighbour. This is the 'lie of necessity', that intends to do good or to restrain evil. The theologians argue over how this fits into a system of ethics, but we see this 'pious deceit' both modelled and commended in the Scriptures (*Exod.* 1:15–21; *Josh.* 2:4–6; *2 Sam.* 17:19–20; *Jer.* 38:24–27; *Heb.* 11:31; *James* 2:25).

LOVE THY NEIGHBOUR

'By the way, did I tell you that I saw John playing the slot machines the other day? Now, I don't want to get him in trouble, but you really ought to know.' The unbridled tongue even uses the truth to spread its poison. This point must not be overlooked: I am not to harm my neighbour in any way whatsoever with my words. If I know something true about you that reflects poorly upon you, I should only raise it through the appropriate legal or ecclesiastical channels, after first attending to the log in my own eye (*Matt.* 7:1–3).

Moses writes in Leviticus 19:15–18:

> You shall do no injustice in court. You shall not be partial to the poor or defer to the great, but in righteous-ness shall you judge your neighbour. You shall not go around as a slanderer among your people, and you shall not stand up against the life of your neighbour: I am the

LORD. You shall not take vengeance or bear a grudge against the sons of your own people, but you shall love your neighbour as yourself: I am the LORD.

Your words, then, must flow out of love for your neighbour, and all talk flowing from malice (idle talk, gossip, slander, be it true or false) is forbidden. You must not say anything against your neighbour that would lower others' opinions of that person. A person's reputation is valuable and ought to be protected. Shakespeare said, 'Who steals my purse steals trash . . . But he that filches from me my good name robs me of that which not enriches him and makes me poor indeed' (*Othello*, III,iii). Love, instead, seeks to cover a multitude of sins, and positively, rejoices in the gifts and graces of others, not in their failings.

The *Westminster Shorter Catechism* says:

Q. 77: What is required in the ninth commandment?

A. The ninth commandment requireth the maintaining and promoting of truth between man and man, and of our own and our neighbour's good name, especially in witness-bearing.

Colossians 3:8–10 says:

But now you must put them all away: anger, wrath, malice, slander, and obscene talk from your mouth. Do not lie to one another, seeing that you have put off the old self with its practices and have put on the new self, which is being renewed in knowledge after the image of its creator.

JARED HOOD

THE BOTTOM LINE

• This commandment is about loving and respecting other people and placing a high value on truth.

• We need to recognize that lying is destructive to relationships and personal maturity. When we lie to protect ourselves it is almost always at the expense of others. When we pass on unconfirmed reports and damaging information about others we are damaging their reputations.

• If we believe that God is a God of truth, then we ought to be committed to speaking the truth as part of our personal growth that reflects the reality that we are his children.

13

THE TENTH COMMANDMENT

*You shall not covet your neighbour's house; you shall
not covet your neighbour's wife, or his male servant,
or his female servant, or his ox, or his donkey, or
anything that is your neighbour's* (Exod. 20:17).

THE MONEY CULT

Adam Phillips, psychoanalyst and author, in a recent
interview for *The Age* said:

We're living in a money cult. In the fourteenth century if
you'd asked people what they wanted they'd have said,
'To be saved.' Now they say, 'To be rich and famous.'

The tenth commandment addresses the cult of money, which
makes the accumulation of material things the measure and
goal of life. In a sign that the nation is increasingly captivated
by money, Australian museums and art galleries are presently
required to put a price on everything in their collections for
insurance purposes. Hence, the heart of the racehorse Phar
Lap is now valued at $1,000,000, Azaria Chamberlain's dress
at $500,000, and the *Hong Hai*, the boat that carried the first
load of Vietnamese refugees to Australia, $1,500,000. Every-
thing must have a dollar value, even down to the flea
collected by Darwin during the voyage of *The Beagle!* This

is the spirit of economic rationalism, all right for business, perhaps, but meaningless when applied to the rest of life.

Discontentment is the primary symptom of coveting. When desires for things take on an importance out of proportion to their proper place, people become dissatisfied with what they have. Much of the advertising we see appeals to these feelings. Hence the car we drive is not luxurious enough; the computer we own could be faster. This goes hand in hand with vanity, so consumers are urged to buy a product 'because you're worth it'.

GOD IS AGAINST GREED!

The tenth commandment expressly prohibits covetousness. Today we would more commonly refer to it as greed. *The Shorter Catechism* explains what is forbidden: 'The tenth commandment forbids all discontentment with our own estate (*1 Cor.* 10:10), envying or grieving at the good of our neighbour (*Gal.* 5:26), and all inordinate motions and affections to anything that is his (*Col.* 3:5).'

The commandment in Exodus 20:17 is repeated in Deuteronomy 5:21, with two small differences. The addition of the word 'land' indicates a recontextualizing of the initial commandment for Israel as she was about to enter into and settle Canaan. The other difference is in the order. In Deuteronomy the commandment begins with a prohibition on coveting a neighbour's wife rather than his house. This suggests that the word *house* in the Exodus 20:17 is to be understood collectively. His most valuable rights then follow in order of importance: first his wife, followed by his slaves and animals. In both places the commandment concludes with a catch-all phrase, 'or anything that is your neighbour's'.

In many ways the commandment can be seen as a summary of the preceding ones because it goes behind the act to the thoughts and motives of the heart. Hence, it is the only commandment which can never be enacted into human law codes. No law can stop people's greed, and no one can witness it, save the individual. Many examples are to be found in Scripture of transgression of this commandment. Achan was greedy for Canaanite gold (*Josh.* 7). David coveted the wife of another man, which then led to the outward act of adultery and murder (*2 Sam.* 11). King Ahab desired his neighbour Naboth's vineyard, which also led to further offences against him (*1 Kings* 21).

If covetousness is prohibited, what attitudes are endorsed by this commandment? The *Shorter Catechism* succinctly answers the above question in the following way: 'The Tenth Commandment requires full contentment with our own condition, with a right and charitable frame of spirit towards our neighbour, and all that is his.' The underlying value of this commandment is contentment. Contented people do not fret or worry at the conditions or limits of God's provision. They are characterized by a thankful spirit, always grateful to God for the supply he has given. And even where there are needs and wants unsupplied, they submit these to God without complaint or grumbling and are pleased to wait upon him for all their requirements. They covet nothing which God has seen fit to give to others but not to themselves.

PROPER ATTITUDES

Possessions, of course, are not wrong in themselves. We own and use material things in order to sustain life and health. But the commandment confronts us at the point where we come to believe that life consists in the abundance of our possessions (*Luke* 12:15).

Neither are all desires evil. Some desires are good and to be cultivated. Paul, for example, speaks of having a desire to depart and be with Christ which is far better (*Phil.* 1:23). But the desires in mind here are those that are ungoverned. To covet means to yearn for something with a view to possessing it. It is an inordinate desire, kindled in the eyes or in the mind, which either envies or begrudges the things our neighbour possesses.

Because this commandment goes to the unseen thoughts and motives of the heart it challenges the modern obsession with 'public image'. The craft of public relations cannot hide from its scrutiny. The current trend of employing spin doctors and image consultants cannot escape its intent. It distinguishes between external hype and actual truth and also critiques all attempts at virtual factuality. The sheer penetrating power of this commandment caught out that 'Pharisee of Pharisees', the apostle Paul. It is significant that he singles it out from all the others when he spoke of the discovery of the power of sin in his own life (*Rom.* 7:7–8.).

The real battleground in a broken world is internal, in the heart and mind. Restoration is not primarily to be found in the environment, gene therapy, or political and socio-economic solutions. Modern man may try educative techniques like counselling and psychotherapy. Help organizations may assist alcoholics and even change drinking habits. Compulsive gamblers may be prevented from gambling by submitting to psychotherapy. But only the power of the Holy Spirit can transform the human heart and bring about lasting change. The commandment makes us aware of our sin, the necessity of a new heart and our need for pardon and forgiveness.

GRASPING SOME OF THE IMPLICATIONS:

The tenth commandment teaches us about God. It tells us that God knows our thoughts, desires, and ambitions as well as our deeds: he alone can legislate for attitudes as well as actions. It tells us that, though man looks on the outward appearance, God looks on the heart (*1 Sam.* 16:7). He knows us better than we do ourselves.

It also teaches us that God is sovereign. When we covet we deny that God is in control of our lives. It is also a denial of his generosity. The covetous person believes that he deserves better and that in some way God has been grudging towards him. It teaches us about the worship of God. Covetousness is a form of idolatry because it elevates something else into the place that only God deserves (*Col.* 3:5). When we ascribe an undue level of importance to any created thing it then becomes the recipient of a worship of which God alone is worthy.

The tenth commandment teaches us about ourselves. It tells us, more than any other, that we are guilty. We may not have been physically standing at the foot of Mount Sinai with the people of Israel, terror stricken by the holiness of God, but we still stand condemned together with them by this same law. Even if we could somehow manage to fend off the censure of the other commandments, this one would catch us out. It is a great leveller of moral topography. It reduces the proud external self-image and uncloaks the whispers of the pharisaic heart: 'God, I thank you that I am not like other men' (*Luke* 18:11).

The commandment shows us that sin lies much deeper than the outward act. The Lord himself, in the Sermon on the

Mount, showed us the radical intent of the law. Lust for a woman may never develop into an outward act, but its presence in the heart is just as capable of sending us to hell as the act of adultery. The sin of anger is as much a breaking of the law as murder, even though no blood has been spilt.

The commandment points us to eternity and the judgment to come by reminding us that, no matter what we long to possess, some day life will be over. All the things that we have desired in life will avail us little in the next, and indeed cannot be taken there with us. All is left behind for someone else to covet! No matter what we have coveted, honour, position, wealth, women, all of these yield before greater and more pressing issues (*Luke* 12:20).

The commandment teaches us to set our hope on God and to crown him King above all earthly things, people or even self (*Matt.* 6:33). Our true happiness is not to be found in possessing material things or in earthly ambitions but in loving and serving God. It claims the whole heart, not just a part of it, because it is so comprehensive.

Above all else, it demonstrates that the law condemns, but cannot cure. No provision is made for relief from its strictures. The commandment cannot save; it can only point to the source of our sin. The law is 'a tutor to lead us to Christ' (*Gal.* 3:24, NKJV). It drives us from Mount Sinai to Mount Zion, from condemnation to grace, from the blood of animal sacrifices to the blood of Jesus Christ (which alone can atone for sin and cleanse the heart), and to faith in him as the way of righteousness.

TONY BIRD

THE BOTTOM LINE

• This commandment speaks about being content with what we have and worshipping the living God rather than people or things.

• Coveting begins in our private thoughts and is always self-centred. It eats away at our happiness, and when outwardly expressed has the potential to do great harm.

• If we consider the level of coveting in our own hearts it will reveal the true spiritual condition more than our outward actions ever would.

• The best cure for coveting is to set our hearts on the God who saves us, who graciously provides our daily needs, and who has an eternity of wonder and joy in store for us.

14

THE TEN COMMANDMENTS IN THE FLOW OF REDEMPTIVE HISTORY

IN THE BEGINNING

The giving of the Ten Commandments by God to Israel at the time of the covenant ceremony on Mount Sinai (*Exod.* 20:1–20) was not the first occasion when he had made known his will. In the case of the Sabbath, its observance was known and practised prior to what transpired at Sinai. God blessed the Sabbath (*Gen.* 2:3), the week of seven days was understood (*Gen.* 27:27), and the Sabbath was observed during the wilderness experience (*Exod.* 16:22–30). The substance of the Ten Commandments had been part of God's law from the very beginning, but sinful humans have always tried to suppress that knowledge (*Rom.* 1:18–23). The basic principles underlying all the Ten Commandments can be seen in the narratives contained in the Book of Genesis.

THE EXODUS AND THE COVENANT

The setting of the Decalogue in Exodus 20 is against a background of redemption from Egypt. It begins with the crucial declaration: 'I am the LORD your God, who brought you out of the land of Egypt, out of the house of slavery.' This is in effect a summary of God's redemptive activity already narrated in the earlier chapters of Exodus. This redemption was an expression of God's love for Israel (*Deut.* 7:7) and the fitting response to it was love to God (*Deut.* 6:5). The Decalogue provides the framework within which that love was to express itself in the maintenance of a true relationship with God and man. Israel had been brought out of slavery in Egypt by the LORD, who had shown great favour and grace to them in their need. There could be no thought that salvation was going to be based on their obedience to God's law. They had not merited, and could not merit, God's favour (*Deut.* 7:7; 9:4–6).

Expressions are used repeatedly to emphasize the link between the Decalogue and God's covenant with Israel. It is called 'testimony' (*Exod* 25:16,21; 40:20; see also *2 Kings* 17:15, NKJV), while the tablets on which it was written are called 'the tablets of the covenant' (*Deut.* 9:9, 11,15), or 'the tablets of the testimony' (*Exod.* 31:18; 32:15; 34:29), or even 'the covenant' (*1 Kings* 8:21). The ark in which they are kept is called 'the ark of the covenant' or 'the ark of the testimony'.

THE ANCIENT NEAR EASTERN BACKGROUND

The Decalogue may be viewed against the extra-biblical treaty pattern of the Ancient Near East. Relationships between nations were often governed by a treaty, imposed upon a subject people by a conquering king. God's law in this setting was an expression of his kingly rule over Israel. Many aspects of the extra-biblical treaties are reflected in details of the Old Testament covenant formula in general, and specifically in relation to the Decalogue. Comparison with them helps to explain various features of the biblical presentation of the

Decalogue. Curses and blessings were an integral part of those treaties and they are embedded in the Decalogue (Second, Third, Fourth, and Fifth Commandments), and are given in more expanded form in Leviticus 26 and Deuteronomy 27–28. When the covenant was broken, even before Moses came down from the mountain, it was remade on the original basis (*Exod.* 34:1, 2). An extra-biblical treaty could be renewed at a later time, and it was common for minor alterations to be made to it when that happened. This helps to explain the variations in the Decalogue in Deuteronomy 5 as compared with Exodus 20.

THE TEN COMMANDMENTS

The nature of God's demands, as expressed in the Ten Commandments, is emphasized by the way in which they were given. While many of the other instructions were given to the children of Israel through Moses as the covenant mediator (*Exod.* 21:1; *Deut.* 5:31; 6:1), the law itself was written with 'the finger of God' (*Exod.* 31:18; *Deut.* 9:10). This signified that the origin and source of the law was God himself, just as the magicians in Egypt had recognized that the plague of insects had come by 'the finger of God' (*Exod.* 9:19).

The Old Testament laws are set out in two different ways. On the one hand there is the directive form given in the Ten Commandments (*Exod.* 20; *Deut.* 5), in which they are given to the individual rather than to the community. They express the basic concepts to which obedience was required. However, the law is also set out in a descriptive form, both in the Book of the Covenant (*Exod.* 20–23) and in Deuteronomy 6–26. The descriptive passages cannot possibly draw out all the implications of the several commandments, but they do provide principles and a framework of understanding that could be applied in a variety of settings. The Old Testament itself gives some examples of how the law was applied, but there is no full account of case law by which we can assess how fully the law was applied, nor the variety of situations to which it was directed.

It has been customary to divide the Decalogue into two tables. The first table of the law has been understood as embracing commandments 1–4, which deal with our relationship to God, while commandments 5–10 form the second table of the law, which deals with relationships with fellow human beings. This division is nowhere made in the biblical text itself. It is recorded that there were two tablets of stone (*Exod.* 31:18; 32:15; *Deut.* 5:22; 9:10), and that they 'were written on both sides; on the front and on the back . . .' (*Exod.* 32:15). No explanation is given of the duplicate tables, but comparison with the extra-biblical treatise suggests that this may have followed a customary practice. One copy was usually placed in the sanctuary of the 'Great King' making the treaty, while the other would be taken by the inferior party and placed in his sanctuary. This customary practice may fit the biblical case, although, in the nature of this case, both copies were placed in the one sanctuary (*Exod.* 40:20).

The Decalogue forms part of the constitutional charter that God provided for Israel the nation. That is to say, God consecrated Israel to himself, applying his universal law to those who were to be his special people. As noted already, all of the basic precepts can be inferred from the creation and patriarchal narratives, and they strongly reinforce the morality of creation. However, it also contains the foundational document setting out the constitution of the nation of Israel. The King who redeemed Israel imposed his requirements on his vassals; transgression of his laws was a serious matter because it was tantamount to rejection of the covenant bond itself. The fact that Israel had 'the whole law' of God was intended to be a witness to the surrounding nations. They were to marvel that Israel's God was so near to his people and that no other nations had such righteous statutes and judgments (*Deut.* 4:6–8).

For the godly in Israel, God's law was a thing of delight; those who meditate on it day and night are pronounced blessed (*Psa.* 1:1-2). The whole of Psalm 119 focuses on the place of God's law in the believer's life, and, by the use of many multi-faceted word-pictures, portrays the law's glorious character. On the other hand, for the ungodly in Israel the law was a burden. The breaking of its stipulations and requirements brought upon the transgressors God's chastisements, punishments, and ultimately, the law's curse (*Deut.* 11:26–29; 29–30; *Isa.* 1:1–18; *2 Kings* 17:5–23; *2 Chron.* 36:15–17).

THE CALL OF THE PROPHETS

The prophets later challenged the people with abuses prohibited in the Decalogue (*Hos.* 4:1–5) and charged the priests with failure to uphold the demands of the law (*Hos.* 4:6–9; *Mal.* 2:1–9). The final prophetic word of the Old Testament is a call to remember the law given at Horeb (*Mal.* 4:4).

OBEDIENCE AND SALVATION

How did Israel think of obedience to the law? Could it possibly bring salvation and forgiveness of sins to the people? The provision of the offerings, especially the sin offering (*Lev.* 4:1–13) and those on the Day of Atonement (*Lev.* 16), proclaimed that the people were unable to meet the law's demands. They stood in need of God's graciously blotting out their sins. The fact that sacrifices were offered on Mount Sinai and that the people were sprinkled with the blood of the covenant proclaimed the necessity of atonement, and the fact that it must come from God's altar (*Exod.* 24:1–8).

The New Testament tells us that all, Jew and Gentile alike, are condemned because they are unable to meet the demands of God's law (*Rom.* 3:19–23). Our salvation can only come through Jesus who kept the law to fulfil all righteousness. He is the sin-bearer and it is only in him that we 'become the righteousness of God' (*2 Cor.* 5:21). The law is our schoolmaster to point us to Christ (*Gal.* 3:24, AV).

ALLAN HARMAN

THE BOTTOM LINE

• The Ten Commandments set out the constitutional charter for God's people to follow as an expression of their love for him and their loyalty to his kingship over them.

• Those who were faithful to God delighted in the inherent goodness of the commandments as a practical guide for life on earth.

• Those who understood the law correctly understood that it was impossible to obey perfectly and therefore turned to the prescribed sacrifices so that God in his mercy would blot out their sin.

• We too ought to delight in the goodness of God's moral law and recognize that we need the mercy of God as revealed in the atoning sacrifice of Jesus.

15

THE MORAL LAW AND JESUS' TEACHING

Many Christians wonder if they are still obliged to keep God's moral commands, such as the Ten Commandments, or whether they are only under the 'law of love'. Jesus answers these questions in the biblical passages discussed in this chapter.

In Matthew 5 (verses 17–20) he explains his own (and his disciples') attitude to the moral commands of the Old Testament; in Matthew 22 (verses 34–40) he explains the place of love in morality.

We are going to talk about the 'moral' law because everything in these two passages of Matthew points to the conclusion that this is what Jesus had in view. In the Sermon on the Mount (*Matt.* 5–7) Jesus explains those moral, relational, and spiritual principles that apply to living under the rule of God; explicitly Jesus speaks about the commandments of the law (5:18), about the need for righteousness (5:20), and about the love that must underlie all our relationships, human and divine (22:37-40). Throughout these passages Jesus connects with us as a moral teacher. For ease of understanding we can gather Jesus' teaching in these two passages into six principles.

GOD'S MORAL LAW IS WHAT JESUS
STANDS FOR (*MATT.* 5:17)

Jesus claims to be the Messiah who has come (his life is a mission from God) not to abrogate God's moral law but rather to 'fulfil' it. What does Jesus mean by fulfilling the law? Again, the context of the Sermon on the Mount helps us to understand his teaching (of which chapter 5 is an excellent example). The chapter gives several examples of what he means. It is true that Jesus fulfilled the law in his own life, but he fulfilled it by giving it the place it deserves in his teaching about the kingdom of God (see the two references to teaching God's moral law in verse 19).

Jesus wants us to understand clearly at the start that part of his life's work was to confirm God's moral law and that he does this in his ethical teaching. Thus, Matthew's Gospel presents Jesus, in the tradition of the rabbis, as a teacher of God's moral law.

GOD'S MORAL LAW IS AS PERMANENT AS
THE CREATION (*MATT.* 5:18)

Jesus summons all his moral authority in speaking about this subject ('Truly, I say to you'; see also verses 20, 22, 28, 32, 34, 39, 44). His authority brings certainty and finality to the subject. Jesus deals with the idea that his coming as the Messiah might somehow mean the disappearance of the moral commands of God. On the contrary, he says, just as heaven and earth will not cease until all God's promises and plans have been fulfilled, so the moral law will not disappear until all that it stands for comes to pass (*Luke* 21:33). So confident is Jesus about this that he engages in what might seem to be an exaggeration by saying that not a jot nor a tittle will pass from the law. These were the smallest elements of the Hebrew script, yet even these cannot be downgraded as a part of God's abiding truth for our human lives. Later Jesus addresses the question of a gradation among the commandments of God.

Clearly, then, Jesus does not take the view that Christians have nothing more to do with the Old Testament moral teaching. Rather, as John Stott says in *The Message of the Sermon on the Mount*: 'the attitude of Jesus to the Old Testament was not one of destruction and of discontinuity, but rather of a constructive, organic continuity.' As a result he reveres those parts of the Old Testament that contain ethical instruction and incorporates them, as we will see next, into his ethics of the kingdom of God.

GOD'S MORAL COMMANDS HAVE AN INTEGRAL PLACE WITHIN THE KINGDOM OF GOD (*MATT.* 5:19)

Having spoken about his own relation to the moral law (verse 17), Jesus now explains the relationship and attitude of his disciples to that law.

People can demote the biblical commandments of God from the Old Testament and teach this point of view to others, or they can honour the commands by keeping them and instructing others to do the same. As far as God is concerned, Jesus says, our reputation among those who live under the rule of God depends on how we rate and speak about God's moral commandments. If a person dishonours them his reputation will be small in the kingdom, but whoever lives out and preaches up God's moral law will receive the accolade of greatness.

Jesus makes a play on the word 'least' by applying it first to the commandments (*the least of these commandments*) and then to people (*least in the kingdom of heaven*). Thus, he shows the direct correlation between anyone's attitude and use of God's law and their standing within the community of disciples. By demoting God's teachings we demote ourselves.

Since Jesus recognizes greater and lesser commandments (again in *Matt.* 22:34–40), he cannot mean that nothing has changed regarding the Old Testament since his coming. But even those commandments that were peculiar to Israel (ceremonial and civil commandments) have the status of Holy Scripture and may contain moral truths that we must still learn from as Christians (*1 Cor.* 9:8–14).

GOD'S MORAL LAW DEMANDS MORE, NOT LESS, FROM US (*MATT.* 5:20)

The Pharisees correctly emphasized practical righteousness, and rightly again connected this with the moral commandments of the Old Testament. But their practice of righteousness focused very much on right actions from a public and social point of view.

Thus they were demonstrative about their alms-giving (*Matt.* 6:2), made loud and long prayers in public places (*Matt.* 6:5), and made it obvious to everyone by their appearance that they were fasting (*Matt.* 6:16).

Instead, Jesus draws attention to the primary need for a pure heart (*Matt.* 5:8) and for inner sincerity in our moral living. This is the righteousness that excels that of the Pharisees; it has just as much to do with the inner person as with our outward life. The Pharisees were dedicated to the externals, Jesus requires the internals of morality (*Luke* 11:39–42).

Otherwise we cannot even enter the kingdom of God. Jesus wants 'more' righteousness, not in a quantitative sense (Pharisaical), but 'more' in a qualitative sense (Christian).

The six examples of kingdom righteousness in Matthew 5 (verses 21–48) illustrate what this means in practice. This is the practical righteousness that Jesus gives as the Messiah who bestows the Holy Spirit and inscribes God's moral laws on the hearts of his people (*Jer.* 31:31–33; *Ezek.* 36:25–27; *John* 3:3–5; *Rom.* 8:1–4).

GOD'S MORAL LAW IS ROOTED IN
LOVING GOD (*MATT.* 22:34–38)

The Pharisees taught right behaviour; Jesus teaches right relationships. This is the world of love, because love is about persons. Behaviour is about other persons and assumes that we already have a relationship with them. And no relationship comes ahead of our relationship with God as the life-giving Lord.

Such is the relationship that we have with God that only a response of total love and commitment to him can express and satisfy it. Notice again how Jesus begins from within by listing the heart, soul and mind in loving God.

This he calls the 'great' and 'first' commandment because without it we cannot proceed to the next one about loving human beings. The command to love God we would call a religious command today, but Jesus shows that there are no valid social ethics in practice without a religious foundation in personally knowing God.

In our post-Christian western societies people imagine that they can engineer ethical communities without religion. Jesus tells us otherwise.

GOD'S MORAL LAW IS ABOUT LOVING OUR FELLOW HUMAN BEINGS (*MATT.* 22:39-40)

Loving God opens the way to loving people, because they are created in God's likeness (*Gen.* 1:26). Claims to religious faith without a respectful attitude to and treatment of other people are worthless, because it is by showing love to other people that we show that we know God (*1 John* 4:19–21).

The standard God demands is loving the other person as we love ourselves. This means responding to the other person in his circumstances in the way we would want him to act if our places were exchanged. This is the meaning of Christ's 'golden rule' (*Matt.* 7:12).

Loving my neighbour means being open to my neighbour's real needs and making an effort to help. The parable of the Good Samaritan teaches me that my neighbour is anyone I meet anywhere who is in need and whom I can help. This requires imagination, sympathy and practical willingness.

The whole moral law of God hangs upon the two love commandments. Jesus does not mean that love replaces law; rather that love is essential to the right kind of law-keeping. Those who pit law (Old Testament) against love (New Testament) have confused two things that differ. Love is about right attitudes to God and other people, without which no one can begin to behave rightly towards either. Even noble social deeds without love are empty (*1 Cor.* 13:3). Love and law-keeping are meant for each other. Love is like the energy that fuels and thrusts the space-ship; God's moral laws are like the trajectory it must follow if it is to fulfil its mission. In the same way Jesus urges on everyone who follows him the need for love *and* law in practice.

DOUGLAS MILNE

THE BOTTOM LINE

• Jesus saw the moral law as unchangeable in nature and as an integral part of kingdom ethics.

• The gospel highlights the importance of the moral law because it brings us back to the heart of what it is about: loving God and those around us.

OLD TESTAMENT
SCRIPTURE REFERENCES

The Ten Commandments are given twice completely: in Exodus 20:1–17 and Deuteronomy 5:1–21. The book of Deuteronomy provides a systematic exposition of the Ten Commandments as follows:

First & Second Commandments	Worship (*Deut.* 12:1–31)
Third Commandment	The sanctity of God's Name (*Deut.* 13:1–14:27)
Fourth Commandment	The Sabbath (*Deut.* 14:28–16:17)
Fifth Commandment	Authority (*Deut.* 16:18–18:22)
Sixth Commandment	Murder (*Deut.* 19:1–22:8)
Seventh Commandment	Adultery (*Deut.* 22:9–23:19)
Eighth Commandment	Theft (*Deut.* 23:20–24:7)
Ninth Commandment	False speech (*Deut.* 24:8–25:4)
Tenth Commandment	Coveting (*Deut.* 25:5–26:29)

The commandments are quoted or alluded to in passages such as:

First Commandment	*Exod.* 34:11–16; *2 Kings.* 17:35; *Psa.* 81:8–10; *Jer.* 7:9; 25:6; 35:15
Second Commandment	*Exod.* 34:17; *Lev.* 19:3-4; 26:1; *Deut.* 27:15; *Ezek.* 18:5–9, 15–17
Third Commandment	*Lev.* 19:12; *Psa.* 24:4; *Hos.* 4:1–2
Fourth Commandment	*Exod.* 23:12; 31:12–17; 34:18–24; 35:2–3; *Lev.* 19:3–4, 30; 20:9; 23:3; 26:2; *Ezek.* 22:8
Fifth Commandment	*Exod.* 21:15, 17; *Lev.* 19:3–4, 32; *Deut.* 2:16; *Jer.* 35:18-19; *Ezek.* 22:7
Sixth Commandment	*Deut.* 27:24–25; *Jer.* 7:9; *Ezek.* 22:6, 9, 12; *Hos.* 4:1–2
Seventh Commandment	*Lev.* 18; 19:11; 20:10–21; *Deut.* 27:20-23; *Prov.* 6:32; *Jer.* 5:8; 7:9; *Ezek.* 18:5–9, 15–17; 22:9–11; *Hos.* 4:1–2
Eighth Commandment	*Lev.* 19:16; *Jer.* 7:9; *Ezek.* 18:5–9, 15–17; *Hos.* 7:1
Ninth Commandment	*Exod.* 23:1-3, 6-9; *Lev.* 19:11; *Psa.* 15:2–4; 24:4; *Prov.* 19:5, 9; 21:28; 24:28; 25:18; *Jer.* 5:2; 7:9; *Hos.* 4:1–2
Tenth Commandment	*Mic.* 2:2

NEW TESTAMENT
SCRIPTURE REFERENCES

The Ten Commandments (in general)	*Matt.* 5:17–18; 22:35–40; *Luke* 18:18–22; *Rom.* 13:8–10
First Commandment	*Matt.* 4:10; 6:24; *John* 20:28; *1 Thess.* 1:9; *1 Tim.* 2:5; *Heb.* 3:12
Second Commandment	*Acts* 17:29; *Rom.* 1:21–25; *1 Cor.* 10:7; 10:14; *1 John* 5:21
Third Commandment	*Matt.* 5:33-37; 12:31–32; *Phil.* 2:9–11; *1 Pet.* 3:15
Fourth Commandment	*Mark* 2:23–28; *Acts* 20:7; *1 Cor.* 16:2; *Heb* 4:1–11; *Rev.* 1:10
Fifth Commandment	*Matt.* 10:37; 15:4–9; *Luke* 2:51; *Eph.* 6:1–2; *1 Tim.* 5:4–8
Sixth Commandment	*Matt.* 5:21-22; *Rom.* 12:19; 13:4; *Eph.* 4:26-27; *1 John* 3:15
Seventh Commandment	*Matt.* 5:27-30; *1 Cor.* 7:2; *Gal.* 5:19; *Eph.* 5:31–32; *1 Thess.* 4:4; *Heb.* 13:4

Eighth Commandment	*Matt.* 25:14–30; *Rom.* 13:7; *Eph.* 4:28; *2 Thess.* 3:6–13; *James* 5:4
Ninth Commandment	*John* 8:44; 16:13; *Col.* 3:9; *Acts* 5:2–3; *Eph.* 4:15, 25; *James* 4:11–12
Tenth Commandment	*1 Tim.* 6:6–10; *Acts* 20:33; *Rom.* 7:7–8; *Col.* 3:5; *Heb.* 13:5; *James* 4:2

FURTHER READING

D. SEARLE	*And Then There Were Nine,* Christian Focus, 2000.
J. DOUMA	*The Ten Commandments,* Presbyterian & Reformed, 1996.
B. H. EDWARDS	*The Ten Commandments for Today,* Day One, 2002.
E. C. REISINGER	*Whatever Happened to the Ten Commandments?* Banner of Truth, 1999.
THOMAS WATSON	*The Ten Commandments,* 1692; Banner of Truth, 1959; frequently reprinted.
W. J. CHANTRY	*God's Righteous Kingdom,* Banner of Truth, 1980.

STUDY GUIDE

THE FIRST COMMANDMENT

1. Discuss some of the ancient and modern substitutes for the one true God of the Bible. Why are these loyalties mistaken (pp. 25–9)?

2. What is the answer to those who want to mix the religions in the world today in the belief that 'the soul of all religions is one' (p. 26)?

3. What are the connections between Jesus' call for total allegiance to himself (*Luke* 14:26) and the exclusive demands of the first commandment (p. 27)?

4. Explain the placing of this commandment as the first in the order of the Ten and how it relates to the other nine (p. 28).

5. What is idolatry, what is its root cause, and why is it so damaging (p. 29)?

6. What is the God-given answer to idolatry and how can we avoid falling into idolatry in a culture that is full of idols (p. 30)?

7. What does it mean to love the Lord our God with all our heart, soul, mind, and strength? How can we encourage and strengthen one another to live like this consistently?

THE SECOND COMMANDMENT

1. What is special about the true God that makes images of him inappropriate (pp. 32–3)?

2. What are some of the lessons and truths about God that the arrangements of the tabernacle teach us (p. 32)?

3. Discuss the theological principle that lies behind the second commandment (p. 33).

4. What are some of the responses we should and should not make to the fact that human beings are God's image in the world (p. 34)?

5. John warns Christians against idols (*1 John* 5:21). What is the meaning of this in the context of John's letter and in our worship and witness today (p. 35)?

6. How does a post-modern mindset work against the requirements of the second commandment (pp. 35–6)

7. What are some of the ways that evangelical Christians might break the second commandment unwittingly (p. 36)?

THE THIRD COMMANDMENT

1. How does this commandment differ from the ninth commandment (pp. 39–41)?

2. What does the name of the Lord stand for (p. 39)?

3. Why does the Lord attach special sanctions to this commandment (pp. 40–1)?

4. What does 'in vain' mean in this commandment (p. 40)?

5. What sin is in view in this commandment (p. 40)

6. Explain and discuss the missionary context of this commandment (p. 42).

7. How does this commandment apply to us and work out for Christians (p. 42)?

THE FOURTH COMMANDMENT

1. Why did God rest when he was able to create everything so effortlessly (p. 45)?

2. What are the two main motivations for keeping the fourth commandment (p. 46)?

3. What reasons can we give for the transfer of the day of rest from the seventh to the first day of the week (pp. 46–7)?

4. What has the example of God as Creator and the example of Jesus as Redeemer to do with the fourth commandment (p. 47)?

5. What would you say to the person who argues that the fourth commandment is restrictive and a denial of enjoyment (pp. 48–9)?

6. What is a balanced attitude to the practice of the Lord's Day (pp. 49–50)?

7. What would you say to someone who claimed that under the gospel we are free from the fourth commandment (p. 48)?

THE FIFTH COMMANDMENT

1. Discuss the relevance of the fifth commandment in the modern world, East and West (p. 52).

2. Does it matter where the fifth commandment comes in the order and organisation of the Ten (pp. 52–3)?

3. What are some of the mistakes parents should avoid in fulfilling this commandment (pp. 53–4)?

4. What does this commandment mean for children (pp. 55–6)?

5. Show how psychology supports the value of this commandment (p. 55).

6. Explain with examples from life how we are obliged to keep this commandment throughout our lives (pp. 56–7).

7. Show how sweeping this commandment is for the whole of life's relationships and responsibilities (p. 58).

THE SIXTH COMMANDMENT

1. What does this commandment have to do with the character and purpose of God (p. 60–1)?

2. How is this commandment related to human beings as image-bearers of God (p. 61)?

3. What defines murder (p. 62)?

4. Is all killing or taking of life forbidden by this commandment (p. 63)?

5. Discuss some of the ways we can break this commandment in everyday life (p. 64).

6. Explain how this commandment helps us to make ethical decisions in beginning-of-life and end-of-life issues (pp. 64–5).

7. Discuss some of the positive ways we can practise this commandment (pp. 65–6).

THE SEVENTH COMMANDMENT

1. Explain the full meaning of the idea of adultery (p. 67).

2. How has the view of marriage and sexual faithfulness changed in the last fifty years (p. 68)?

3. How does the Word of God help us to grasp the seriousness of this sin (pp. 69–70)?

4. Why should a marriage involve a public ceremony (pp. 70–1)?

Study Guide

5. Discuss the larger spiritual message of marriage (p. 71).

6. How do the first four commandments help us to think about our marital relationship and responsibilities (p. 72)?

7. Discuss the range of sexual relationships and activities that this commandment sheds light on in the modern context (p. 72).

THE EIGHTH COMMANDMENT

1. Give examples of ways our consumer society makes it difficult for us to keep this commandment (pp. 74–5).

2. What does this commandment urge us positively to do (pp. 75–6)?

3. Discuss examples of stealing in the ancient and modern worlds (pp. 76–7).

4. Explain the moral principles that underlie this commandment (p. 77).

5. What are some of the responses Christians should make to this commandment (p. 78)?

6. What are some of the behavioural responses this commandment can help us to avoid in modern life (p. 79)?

7. Discuss the relevance of this commandment to plagiarism, hostage-taking, the sin of unbelief, and not returning borrowed items.

THE NINTH COMMANDMENT

1. Why does this commandment clash with our post-modern culture (p. 81)?

2. What was the context of this commandment and why is it important for every society today (p. 82)?

3. Discuss some of the biblical passages that endorse our efforts to practise a proper legal system (p. 83).

4. What is the fundamental truth underlying the ninth commandment (pp. 83–4)?

5. Discuss some of the ways people commonly break this commandment (p. 84).

6. Can we ever justify lying (p. 85)?

7. What does this commandment have to do with our everyday conversations, especially about other people (pp. 85–6)?

THE TENTH COMMANDMENT

1. What is another word for coveting and what is entailed in it (pp. 89–90)?

2. What is special about this commandment and what is its connection to the other nine (pp. 90–1)?

3. Look at some examples of greed from the Scriptures and discuss what we can learn from these examples (pp. 92–3).

4. What is the answer to greed and how can this remedy be applied (p. 90)?

5. What are the deeper needs that this commandment points to (pp. 91–3)?

6. What are some of the lessons taught by this commandment about our relationship to God (p. 92)?

7. What are some of the truths taught by the tenth commandment about ourselves (pp. 92–3)?

DOUGLAS MILNE